52 Bedtime Stories for Grownups

Nostalgia From The 1940's and '50's

Laura Martin-Palmatier

To my sisters who helped bring the country stories to life
And
To the Northside guys who added zest to the city stories:
Gene Craver, Dan Tallet, Don Ross, and Bub Burley
Thank you all!

TABLE OF CONTENTS

The Box Camera 1

A Sleigh Full of Valentines 6

The Best Storm Ever 10

Trapping 15

Underwear Buttons 18

Salt Sacks, Sugar Sacks, etc. 22

The Bucket-A-Day Stove 25

The Alcohol Iron 28

The Yo-Yo Man 31

To Make A Bed 34

May Basket 37

Horse Medicine 40

Buzz Saws 44

A Family Graduation 47

Freebies 52

The Hay Wagon 57

Bicycle Ringelivia 60

Everything But The War 63

Polio! 67

When The Clock Stopped 71

Glamour Girls 74

Circus Worker 77

Elderberry Tattoos 81

The Refined Look 84

Welcoming the Light 89

Shopping at Jones's 92

Stick-and-Bread Dough Batons 96

Potato Picking 100

The Sunshine Box 104

The Engagement 108

The Cure 111

The Umbrella 114

Apples 117

When Snow White Came to Town 121

The Hobo Jungle 125

Operator 128

Cows and Apples 133

County Fair 136

Thank You, Patti Page! 141

Singin' for the Good Ol' Lifebuoy 145

Boiler Inspector 148

Hand Me Downs 151

Autograph Books 154

Stealing From Sears Roebuck 158

Burma-Shave 162

The Scooter Ride 165

Clothesline Tents 169

Punch Boards 172

A Kindergarten Education 175
First Aid 179
The Christmas Ring 181
The Lesson of
the Flashlight 188

THE BOX CAMERA

In nineteen forty-two, World War II was blazing on every front. At school, we practiced air raid drills, squatting in the hall and covering our heads with our arms until the all-clear whistle sounded. Boys drew swastikas on their book covers, just to be disgusting. At night, I'd lie in bed between the sleeping twins, staring into the darkness, worrying about what I'd do if I heard a plane or worse yet, heard a bomb We needed to fear the Germans; I was only six, but I knew that.

On the other hand, there was Gus.

A bachelor, he had emigrated from Heidelberg and bought a farm near us soon after World War I. Gus was short and smiley, with pointy ears, a shiny baldhead, and a gentle face. If he hadn't been our neighbor, he'd have slipped into a storybook and become a gnome.

Every New Year's Day, we'd invite Gus to our house for dinner. A few days before, Dad would tuck ration books in his bib overalls pocket and go to town to buy a roast of beef.

"Poor old batch," my father would say. "He's all alone over there with just a dog for company."

On New Year's Day, my sisters and I started watching for Gus around eleven o'clock in the morning. We'd see the top of his head, clad in a tan knit hat, crest our snow-covered hill, and then we'd see the rest of him, marching vigorously up our road, dressed in his tan winter jacket and heavy tan coveralls, puffing his breath into the cold winter air. His German Shepard, Jim, trotted beside him. Under his arm, Gus carried a gift for our family, wrapped in a grocery bag. For years he brought a gallon of maple syrup, made from the sap of his own sugar maples.

The year that I was six, I watched him coming up our hill, as usual, carrying his grocery bag. When he came in the house, he took off his coat and put it on my parents' bed, just off the kitchen, along with his gift.

Gus liked to sit near us children at the table so he could polish our manners: "Pass the dishes to the left, now," he'd say, or, "Break your bread, and butter it one piece at a time, now."

I didn't need Gus to monitor my manners; my mother took care of that, but I liked his attention, and my sisters did, too.

We spent the afternoon, sitting around the parlor stove in the living room, Gus and my father toasting their feet in their heavy woolen socks while they discussed the weather, their cows, and spring planting. The twins and I knelt on the blue linoleum and dressed our Christmas paper dolls.

Finally, Gus said, "Let's all sing, now," and my sister, Bea, moved to the piano. Gus sang Christmas songs in German—O Tannenbaum, and Stille Nicht, Stille Nicht in his high, thin tenor.

On that New Year's Day his voice sounded sad and plaintive, and even though the piano played under Bea's nimble fingers and Gus continued to sing, heaviness crept into our living room.

"Do you miss Germany, Gus?" Dad asked quietly.

Bea stopped playing, and Bev and I stopped dressing our paper dolls.

"I miss my home," Gus said, "My mother is old. I worry that she might be cold or hungry, but I can't write or call her, and even if I could, how could I send her food or money for the heat?" He was quiet.

A chunk of wood settled in the stove.

"Maybe, over there, they're saying, "He's a draft dodger. He's a traitor," Gus continued. "I'm not. I fought for Germany in the last war, but now I'm too old to fight on any side. Besides, I'm a citizen of this country."

Gus shrugged. "But that is war," he said.

When it was time for Gus to go home that day he handed his gift to my mother.

"I brought you something different this year," he told her. "You open it, now."

Mother reached into the bag and took out a box camera.

"Why, Gus!" she said. "I can't accept this. It's too much—it's way too expensive."

"No, you keep it," he said. "The government says I must give it away or turn it over to them."

He smiled at my mother. "So! Look here at these young faces. Think of all the pictures you can take!"

My mother turned the camera over in her hands.

"Gus, if you ever need to take a picture, I'll bring it right over," she said. "Just tell me if you need it."

"I have enough pictures," he told her. "Now, you take some."

It was time for Jim the dog to perform, the way he did every New Year's Day.

"You tell these girls how old you are, Jim," Gus said.

I held my breath and waited, hoping Jim would get it right.

"Woof! Woof! Woof! Woof?"

"Oh, now, Jim, you forgot you had a birthday," Gus said.

"Woof!"

"Good dog! Oh, good dog!" the twins and I said. "Good dog!"

Gus took his change purse from his pocket and gave us each fifty cents.

Then he put on his hat and coat and slipped into his boots and mittens.

The twins and I stood at the window and watched Gus and Jim walk briskly down our road in the gathering darkness.

My mother put the camera on the top pantry shelf, the place reserved for our most valuable and precious possessions. That camera was the only one she ever owned, and whenever she could afford a roll of film, she took pictures of her family.

Now, those photographs that document our early lives are priceless to my sisters and me. When I look at them, I often think of our kind German neighbor and that wonderful wartime New Year's Day.

TRIVIA

Questions:

1. The swastika is an ancient symbol, about three thousand years old. The word is derived from Sanskrit. What is the true meaning of the symbol?

2. Einstein immigrated to the U.S. in 1933. What was his native country?

3. What was the name of Hitler's girlfriend/wife?

Answers:
1. Life, power, strength, and good luck
2. Germany
3. Eva Braun

A SLEIGH FULL OF VALENTINES

Valentines Day in Upstate New York offers three types of weather--cold and blustery, cold and stormy, or cold, blustery and stormy. Grownups pay attention to such dreary selections; little children don't.

Their minds are focused on bright valentines, a party at school in the afternoon, and a bag full of two kinds of candy hearts, the red cinnamon flavored ones and the pastel colored confections with little notes—"Love you" and "Sweet girl"-- and lovely valentines to carry home. Valentines Day is red, white, sweet, and fun!

For a few winters when I was small, the school people who focused on "dreary" realized the winter weather was so terrible, and the school bus was so prone to sliding into the ditch, the prudent choice would be to hire my father to deliver three families to the main road every morning and take them home every afternoon.

Dad sharp-shod Daisy, a black, and Dusty, a grey, so they wouldn't slip on the ice and snow. Then, he built a sledge--a low box with runners, and boards laid across the box for seats. He put hay in the bottom in a futile attempt to keep our feet warm, and covered us completely with three new horse blankets. We were ready! My sisters and the older neighbor boys muttered and complained. The boards that Dad had placed across the box for seats were fastened so they couldn't slide from side to side, but they slid forward and backward, depending on whether the team was going up hill or down.

The girls slid into the boys, and the boys slid into the girls, and that made everybody mad. Besides, they were under the horse blankets with kids of the opposite sex. How embarrassing could life get? Of course, they felt like country hicks, getting on the bus with hay on their snow pants and boots, and wafting the odor of horses.

Jenny, Sukey, and I loved our morning and afternoon rides. We knelt in the hay and used our seat for a table. In the dim light that crept around the edges of the horse blanket, we played games, colored in coloring books, and practiced writing numbers. Before Valentines Day we drew lopsided paper hearts and colored them.

A few days before our party, we boarded the sledge with bags of valentines. The excitement was ramping up! Each of us had addressed our cards in our best printing for everyone in the class.

Oh, the parties we had! Mothers sent valentine cookies, fresh apples, extra candy, and paper napkins.

After we were well energized from the sweets, we each claimed our decorated shoeboxes filled with valentines, and we pored over them as if they were notes from the queen.

When it was time to go home, our teacher gave each of us a grocery bag.

"Put your valentines in the bag, and don't take them out until you get home," she said. I'll call that warning number one.

That afternoon, when our bus pulled up next to the sledge, Fanny and Dusty were standing, heads down, tails to the wind, their backs covered with snow. Dad stood tall and tough, holding the reins in his mittened hands, his ear flaps down, and his coat collar pulled up around his neck. The fierce gusts had turned his face as red as one of our crayons.

We boarded the sledge, and Dad covered us with the horse blankets. Then he said, "You kids leave your valentines in the bags. Don't take them out until you get home."

That was warning number two.

Being a father of eleven and a countryman, Dad had plenty of experience with small children, holiday parties, and February weather.

Cuddled under the horse blankets, listening to the horses' harnesses jingling, and bursting with holiday excitement, Jenny and Sukie and I helped ourselves to candy from our bags. Then, Jenny said, "We could show each other our best valentines."

How could we do that? Our cards were inside dark paper bags under the dark horse blankets. We couldn't tell one valentine from another.

Despite the teacher's warning and Dad's warning, we had no choice. We laid all our valentines out on our makeshift table, showing each other the ones from our best friends, the funniest, the most beautiful, the ones from our teachers.

Then the team stopped. We were at Jenny's house! Before we could gather our valentines, someone pulled off the horse blanket. One mighty gust of wind picked up our valentines and sent them soaring and pin wheeling across the snow.

Sukey and Jenny began to cry. The older siblings frowned at us. Dad calmly held the team.

"You big kids get out and get the valentines," he said.

Glowering at us little ones, the big sisters and brothers set off through the wind and snow, sinking into the drifts, lunging clumsily at our precious cards.

When all of them were retrieved, the older ones did their best to decipher the kindergarten, first, and second grade writing—"who has a Brenda in their class?" Soon Jenny hopped off the sledge with her bag of valentines. Sukey and I clutched our bags in our mittened hands.

Thank goodness for big sisters and brothers. Thank goodness for patient dads!

And hooray for Valentines Day!

TRIVIA

Questions:

1. How many valentines are sent every year in this country?

2. Name two symbols of Valentines Day

3. St. Valentine's skull can still be seen. Where is it?

Answers:

1. A billion

2. Hearts, cupids, doves, chocolates

3. A museum in Rome

THE BEST STORM EVER

According to my parents and the school, it was the worst storm ever, but if you asked my sisters and me, it couldn't have been better.

We were four gloomy sisters when we walked down our dirt road to meet the bus that day, and it was our mother's fault. Here we were, dressed like darn Eskimos, sweating in our snowsuits, hats, boots, and mittens on a sunny, balmy late February morning. Geese flew overhead, chickadees called from the treetops, and the snow in our road had dissolved into a sea of mud. Anybody with eyes and ears could tell it was spring, except for our mother.

"February is never spring," she said. "When it's time to take off your winter clothes, I'll let you know."

She had no sense of fashion, we muttered. Why would she care that we'd be getting on the bus with kids who were dressed appropriately for spring? I was still wearing my long brown stockings, for heaven's sake, and everybody else was wearing ankle socks. We vented our frustrations as we stomped along on the tops of the remaining snow banks to keep the mud off our boots.

We didn't dare to disobey our mother. She was a calm, quiet woman, and we loved her, but at times like this, we felt as if we were in a game of "Simon Says". Simon Says do this. Simon Says do that. Mom says do this. Mom says do that.

As soon as school started that day, Mrs. Roach pulled the shades to keep the sun off the blackboard and our eight-year-old minds on our lessons. At lunchtime when she raised the shades, the sun had disappeared and the air was white with fast-falling snow. We couldn't see the sky, the sidewalk, or the church next door. All we could see was the snow.

Mrs. Roach didn't pull the shades again. She tried to keep us interested in our schoolwork, but we kept turning toward the windows, watching the snow falling in dense white sheets. Mrs. Roach kept looking, too. Finally, she put down her book and chalk, and the whole class sat in silence, watching the storm.

Just before dismissal time, the principal's calm, authoritative voice crackled over the loudspeaker.

"The buses," he said, "Will not be running this afternoon. All bus children will stay in town with relatives or friends, or they can stay here at the school. Older children should take charge of younger brothers and sisters."

What a relief! My sister, Shirley, a seventh grader, would have to figure out what to do. Soon she came to collect me, trailing Bev and Bea, my ten-year-old twin sisters.

"Get your snowsuit on," she said. "And your boots and hat and mittens."

As I walked to the coatroom, an image of us grumbling girls, walking down the hill that morning flashed through my mind. Mother had been oh-so-right! I was more than glad to bundle up before I joined my sisters.

"Where are we going?" I whispered, gripping Shirley's coat sleeve.

"To Aunt Ella's," Shirley said.

"Who's Aunt Ella?"

"She's Dad's aunt-by-marriage. She married Grandpa's brother, but he's dead now."

"What's she like?"

"Well, I don't know! I only met her once! Look, would you rather stay with a stranger?"

I shook my head.

Shirley made sure we were bundled up, and then she marched us out into the storm. Hand-in-hand, we made our way through knee-deep drifts on Main Street to a narrow door between the five-and-ten and the Grand Union. Inside, we felt our way up a dark flight of stairs and along a hallway. Shirley knocked softly on a door.

When the door opened, a tiny white head popped out.

"Oh, you came!" she said. "I was hoping you would!" She burst out of her apartment, eyes twinkling and cheeks glowing, and sprinted across the hall to bang on another door.

"Mrs. Brooks!" she yelled. "Mrs. Brooks! They're here! We've got company!" (Mrs. Brooks, Aunt Ella explained between shouts, was hard of hearing.)

Another tiny head, wrapped in black braids, appeared.

"Bless my soul! Oh, bless my soul!" said Mrs. Brooks. "We'll make popcorn and cocoa and play cards and string beads . . ."

"And fix supper!" said Aunt Ella. "And make up my spare bed!"

As soon as we children single-filed into Aunt Ella's dollhouse-sized apartment, we made a beeline to the big front window. We looked down onto Main Street, where the town's lone traffic light flashed its colors. The street lamps shone softly through the falling snow, and the neon sign above the Three Bear Inn across the street winked off and on.

We were fairly bursting with excitement. For us country children, this was big city living!

Aunt Ella made sure we ate a proper supper, and then cleared the table for a game of "Old Maid". Later, Mrs. Brooks brought a big box of old costume jewelry from her apartment, and we carefully sorted and restrung the beads, speaking politely to Aunt Ella, and yelling in Mrs. Brooks' good ear.

By the time we finished with our popcorn and cocoa it was ten o'clock, but Aunt Ella said we could sleep late the next day.

We wore our fashionable new jewelry to bed that night. I settled down between the twins in the double bed, filled with contentment, with all my beautiful beads lumped around my neck.

Late the next afternoon, the bus came to take us home. We said good-bye to Aunt Ella and Mrs. Brooks and promised to come back often, and we did. That night in Aunt Ella's apartment was the beginning of a warm, strong friendship that lasted for many years.

Aunt Ella and Mrs. Brooks have passed away now, and the building that housed the Grand Union, the five-and-ten, and the apartments has been razed.

Still, whenever I pass through that little town at night and see the lone traffic light flashing, the streetlights glowing, and the neon sign from the Three Bear Inn winking off and on, I think of Aunt Ella and Mrs. Brooks and our wonderful, stormy night in the town.

TRIVIA

Questions:

1. Almost every small town had a grocery store and a five and dime. Name two other stores or public buildings that were common on Main Street

2. For kids whose families had telephones, what number would they have dialed to call their parents and tell them they had to stay in town?

3. Studded tires and snow tires were still in the future. What did drivers of the forties use to get their cars through the snow?

Answers:

1. Bank, library, feed store, hardware store, doctor's office

2. "0". All calls went through the operator

3. Chains

TRAPPING
(A city story by Jon)

I can't remember how my friend, Bubby, and I got into the trapping business. I suppose the idea came to us when we were trying to figure out how to make some easy money. We were around fourteen at the time, starting to look at girls, and desperately in need of funds.

I can't remember how we got our traps, and I can't recall how we sold the pelts. I'm not even sure we caught anything. Bubby can't remember, either. We both remember in great detail, though, the day we stole the traps.

First, let me tell you some truths about trapping.

No cold is more penetrating than dead-of-winter river cold, when hoar frost clings to the trees along the banks and shrouds the frozen water in a bone-numbing fog. No cold is more penetrating than six-in-the-morning cold, when a young boy must force himself out of his warm bed and into the world to tend his traps. But that's business.

There's another truth about trapping. Other people run trap lines, too, and they don't appreciate a couple of young know-nothing kids, setting traps in their territory. A seasoned trapper handles the situation by pulling out the offending traps and keeping them.

One bitter February morning, I rolled out of my warm bed, as usual, bundled myself up, and walked to the bridge to join Bubby for our five-mile morning frolic along the frigid Chenango River to check our traps. Hunched down into our coats, our mittened hands stuffed in our pockets for extra warmth, we trudged along silently until we arrived where we had set our traps.

We couldn't believe our eyes! Our traps were gone! Somebody had stolen our traps!

We were outraged as only two teenaged boys could be. On the way home, we forgot how cold we were as we marched along, snorting and snarling like a couple of young bulls. Then we devised a plan. If somebody had stolen our traps, we'd just steal somebody else's. Fair is fair.

The next morning, I practically bounded out of bed. I met Bubby on the bridge and we went striding along the riverbank, looking for traps. We must have been a strange sight. I hadn't gained much height or weight at that time; I was about five-feet-six and weighed around a hundred pounds. Bubby, on the other hand, was well over six feet, but he was as thin as a pencil. Mutt and Jeff on a business trip along the frigid river.

Then we came upon a trap line.

I helped myself to as many traps as I could, slinging them over my shoulders and around my neck, letting the wet, smelly contraptions rest against the only coat I owned—my wool mackinaw school jacket. Then I waited for Bubby to load up.

Bub was wearing a white pullover Army surplus parka, hardly suited for carrying traps. He hesitated. He couldn't get the dirty, wet traps near that jacket—not the outside or the inside of it. There was just one thing to do--he tucked his shirt and parka into his pants and stuffed the cold steel traps inside, next to his skin.

He barely got loaded up when we heard the shots . . .
Boom! Boom!

Somebody was shooting at us!

We took off, running as fast as we could, slipping and
sliding along the frozen riverbank.

Behind us, we heard it again . . .Boom! Boom!

My traps were weighing me down. I flung them aside
and picked up speed.

Poor Bubby! He couldn't get rid of his traps. He
couldn't stop to pull his shirt and parka out of his pants,
and he couldn't pull the jumble of traps out of the top of
his parka. His long legs flying, he raced next to me, putting
distance between the gun and us.

When we didn't hear it anymore, Bubby stopped and
dumped the traps from under his shirt. Then he showed me
his chest. It was rubbed raw.

That was the day we gave up our trapping business.

TRIVIA

Questions:

1. Name one animal that is trapped for its fur
2. Why is trapping done in the dead of winter?
3. Name one item of clothing that is made of fur

Answers:
1, Muskrat, mink, fox . . .
2. The animals' fur is heavier
3. Hats, coats, stoles, mittens, muffs

UNDERWEAR BUTTONS

Even during World War II when rubber was rationed, there should have been a way to hold up underwear that didn't require buttons. The embarrassment and inconvenience we children endured was a bigger sacrifice to the war effort than most people realized.

I was in kindergarten when I lost my undies because of a popped button.

"Now, who can count all the way to one hundred?" the teacher asked.

I frantically waved my hand. I could hardly wait to get in front of the class and rattle off those numbers.

One-two-three-four—I got all the way to ten before I saw a button roll across the floor and felt my unmentionables slipping. I put my hands on my straight, baby hips and tried to hold my panties against me, but it was no use.

Down they came. My homemade underpants made from cloth sugar sacks settled around my shoe tops. I didn't know what a person should do in such a situation. Should I pull them back up and mince back to my chair? Should I step out of them and carry them away in my hand? I simply stood there blushing until the teacher came, hiked up my undies, and secured them with a safety pin.

"Just go on with your counting," she said quietly.

It was too late. I was so rattled I couldn't think of how to count at all.

I went back to my chair and sat down.

Still, I was luckier than Gloria.

In May of our kindergarten year, the teacher helped us make a Maypole. We invited all the grades in the elementary school, as well as our parents, to come and watch us skip around, holding crepe paper streamers and singing spring songs while the teacher played the piano.

We skipped. She played. Everything was going along just the way we had practiced until Gloria stopped. Then we all stopped and stared. There went the button, rolling across the stage, and there went her underpants, sliding over her knees and landing in a heap on top of her shoes.

Gloria was a shy blond child, the tallest girl in our class. Her dresses were always way too short; in fact they looked like she outgrew them while her mother was still stitching them together. Poor Gloria! There she was, in a dress barely covering her buns, her panties around her ankles, and her face so red it looked ready to catch fire.

Like me, she had no idea of what to do next, and like me, she simply stood there, steeped in embarrassment, waiting for help.

Our teacher, armed with her handy safety pin, came up on the stage, placed herself between Gloria and our audience, slid Gloria's underwear up, and pinned them.

"We'll just go on with our singing now," she told us. She sat down at the piano, and we began to dance around the Maypole again, including poor Gloria.

Sometimes, even when buttons didn't pop, they caused trouble.

Early in the spring of my seventh year, my sisters and I decided to walk to Sunday school, about three miles away.

The sun was shining and the snow was melting that morning. We left our house wearing ankle socks, dresses, and jackets. After all, it was spring! No hats or mittens for us!

We hadn't gone far when we began to notice the sharpness of the wind. We pulled up our coat collars and stuffed our hands in our pockets as we picked up our pace. Our noses felt numb and our bare knees turned purple. It was cold!

We warmed ourselves at Sunday school and started home.

When we got to our road, Bea said, "I have to pee."

She unbuttoned her underpants, squatted, and took care of her business.

She fumbled and fumbled with the button, but her hands were so cold and stiff she couldn't get it through the buttonhole.

I tried. Bev tried. Bea blew on her fingers and tried again. We were just too cold to handle something as small as that darn button.

"Oh, never mind," Bea said testily. "If you two can't help me I might as well take them off."

Stuffing her underwear in her pocket, she practically flew up the hill and into the warmth of our kitchen. When her hands were finally warm, she slipped into her underwear and buttoned them right there in the kitchen, in front of our whole family.

Who could blame her for her lack of modesty? Who could blame Gloria for disrupting our play? Who could blame me for forgetting how to count? No one! It wasn't our fault!

I lay the blame at the feet of the federal government. It definitely crossed the line when it took away our underwear elastic.

TRIVIA

Questions:

1. Boys didn't use buttons on their underwear during the war, and they didn't use elastic. How did they hold up their skivvies?

2. Name three items that were rationed during the war

3. Practically everybody planted gardens during the war. What were they called?

Answers:

1. Snaps

2. Sugar, shoes, coffee, gasoline, tires . . .

3. Victory gardens

SALT SACKS, SUGAR SACKS, FLOUR SACKS, AND FEED SACKS

In 1942, more than three million Americans were spiffing up their homes and wardrobes with cotton sacks that had contained flour, sugar, salt, and livestock feed. People in more comfortable circumstances than my family even got dog food in cotton sacks, and "roll-your-own" tobacco in cotton pouches.

Oh, the joys of those sacks! The possibilities!

Tobacco pouches were used to hold jacks and other game pieces, sorted buttons, and harvested flower seeds.

The finely woven white cotton salt and sugar sacks were perfect for making panties and training pants, and the string that had secured the tops of the bags could be transformed into crocheted lace to trim panty legs. Any printing on the fabric was washed out or bleached in the sun. I can't even estimate how many pairs of panties and training panties my mother made in her quest to cover the bottoms of her ten little girls.

There's a story in our family about the twins during their potty training time.

They'd rush outside on some important mission, and when one twin wet her pants she stopped, stepped out of them, and flung them aside. Then the other twin did the same.

When my father or an older sister walked down the road, they returned with a handful of little white panties.

Depending on the size of the sack, of course, that beautiful, fine cotton could also be transformed into a slip, a special handkerchief, a soft bandage, or an embroidered sampler.

Flour sacks were heavier and coarser. They were perfect for towels, heavy aprons, and backings for quilts. The printing on those sacks was difficult, and sometimes impossible to remove. My mother owned a slip once that proudly advertised "GLF", our local feed store, in blue flowery letters on the back. She said that didn't matter; it was a nice, heavy winter slip, and who'd ever see it?

Most sacks from the feed store were printed in a colorful selection of florals, stripes, border prints, and even polka dots, as tempting as the fabrics displayed in any store or catalog. Some were marked with patterns for aprons, and even dolls and stuffed animals. Farmers came into the feed store and shopped, not just for the grains and corn meal, but for a certain pattern or color of feed sack that their wives wanted to make into a dress with a sweetheart neckline, or a blouse, or perhaps a broomstick skirt, or curtains, pillow cases, a quilt, or a table covering.

They came in a standard size, 36"x36". Four sacks would make a dress if the fabric pattern didn't require matching. Five sacks were better, because they'd make a more generous dress without pinching and pulling.

In 1943, the War Production Board got involved with those wonderful, free sacks, and they standardized their sizes. Henceforth, they'd hold two, five, ten, twenty-five, fifty, and one hundred pounds.

Maybe the government thought those new regulations were important, but for the three million Americans who proudly wore those transformed feed sacks and decorated their homes with them, it probably didn't matter at all.

TRIVIA

Questions:

1. Name a popular brand of sewing machine that was used to transform those feed sacks.

2. Name two catalogs that women could study to keep up on the latest fashions.

3. Certain clothing accessories had to be purchased— shoes, for instance. When ordering shoes from a catalog, how did you find your proper shoe size?

Answers:

1. White, Singer, New Home . . .

2. Sears Roebuck, Montgomery Ward, Spiegel

3. You placed your foot on an outline of a foot in the catalog, and the numbers on the side determined your length and width.

THE BUCKET-A-DAY STOVE
(A city story by Jon)

Many people live out their lives without finding their ideal jobs. I found mine when I was eleven years old, and my parents assigned me the task of tending the bucket-a-day stove.

True to their name, these efficient little stoves demanded just one bucket of coal a day and they provided all the hot water an average household of the nineteen forties needed. They were easy to tend—somebody had to go down to the basement once a day, clean out the ashes, make sure there were enough embers to ignite the next bucket of coal, shut the door, and come back upstairs. Even an eleven-year-old boy could do that.

My first few days on the job went smoothly. After I shook down the ashes, there were always plenty of red embers left to start my next bucket of coal, so on a good day, I could complete the job in five minutes and come back up to the kitchen.

Then, my imagination started to perk, and instead of coming right upstairs, I began to spend some time looking into the stove, mesmerized by the shimmering, glowing embers, and thinking . . .

Some night, I thought, there wouldn't be enough embers left, and I'd need to start a blazing, crackling new fire. I could see myself, crumpling the newspapers, building a little tent of the kindling, lighting the match, and gradually adding the coal. I had watched my father start fires, so I knew how to do it, even though such an endeavor was definitely not part of my job description. Every night I went down to the basement with hope in my heart, but the bucket-a-day purred along, and there were always enough embers to start the next bucket of coal.

The temptation finally got to be too much. If those embers wouldn't die, I'd make them die! I'd pour water on those stubborn coals and give myself a reason to start my dream fire.

An old black sink stood in the far corner of the basement. It wasn't used much, except for when my father cleaned his paintbrushes. He hadn't painted anything in ages, and there was no reason for me to think the old tomato can on the edge of the sink would contain anything other than water. It looked like water. I smelled its contents to be sure. It was odorless, like water. Well then, water it was!

I opened the door of the stove and threw the contents of the can onto the fire. It was paint thinner.

Boom!

The explosion happened so fast I never saw it. In the silence that followed, I watched the flakes of asbestos and particles of dust float down from the pipes all over the basement, covering my plaid mackinaw jacket, the sink, the floor, the bucket-a-day—covering everything

The stovepipe from the bucket-a-day fed into our main chimney, and its entrance, along with the stovepipe for the furnace, was secured with asbestos filler. That's how it was before the explosion. Now, both stovepipes hung limp and loose, and the basement was filled with smoke.

Slowly, I walked upstairs.

My grandmother, who lived with us, was in the kitchen.

"Did you hear that explosion?" she asked. "It sounded like it was out on the bridge."

I didn't tell her I'd heard it, all right. I'd seen it and smelled it, and all that was left for me to do was to try to explain it to my father.

He went down to the basement, and with plenty of huffing, and not a little cussing, he secured the stovepipes to the chimney again. Then, he started a new fire in the bucket-a-day.

Then he fired me.

TRIVIA

Questions:

1. What were two other names for "the coal bucket"?
2. Roughly how much coal could it hold?
3. Name one size of coal

Answers:

1. A hod or a scuttle

2. About five gallons

3. Chestnut coal, stove coal, pea coal, egg coal . . .

THE ALCOHOL IRON

During the nineteen forties, most folks in small towns, and those who lived on paved roads, were enjoying the benefits of electricity. Country families like ours, however, were still stumbling around after dark with kerosene lanterns and lamps, milking cows by hand, and building roaring fires in mid-summer to heat water for laundry and bathing, and heating irons for pressing clothes.

My sister, Marge, was grown up and married when I was still a kid. Much as she loved the convenience of electricity in her own house, she squirmed with guilt when she thought of her mother out there in the country, still living in the dark ages. If she could think of any fandangled contraption that would make her mother's life easier (or brighter) she'd rush to supply it.

One evening, she and her husband arrived at our house with an alcohol iron.

"Go find something to iron, Mom," she said, "And Ivan and I will show you how to use this."

Mother found three bandana handkerchiefs. She placed a bath towel over the oilcloth on the kitchen table, and Marge and Ivan proceeded to sell Mother on the wonders of the iron.

"Don't bother to get a holder to cover the handle, the way you do when you heat the irons the stove," Marge said. "The handle on this doesn't even get hot."

Before Mother could respond, Ivan proceeded with his instructions.

"N-n-n-now, first you f-f-f-fill this t-t-t-t-tank here with al-al-al-cohol," Ivan instructed. Using a small funnel, he filled the round tank at the back of the iron.

"B-b-b-but not t-t-t-too full."

"How will I know when it's just enough, Ivan?" Mother asked.

"You just kinda know, Mom," Marge said. "You'll get used to it."

"N-n-n-now, you take this little p-p-p-pump and pump some air into it, r-r-r-right here," Ivan said, He attached the pump to the iron and pushed its handle up and down.

"Now, how much air would it take?" Mother asked cautiously.

"Oh, we don't know," Marge said. "I used this iron all the time before we got electricity, and I never even thought about it. You just know."

Ivan was moving on.

"N-n-n-now," he said, his bright blue eyes sparkling like a kid on the Fourth of July, "G-g-g-get me a m-m-m-match and I'll light 'er up."

Dad handed Ivan a match and stepped quickly away from the table.

"Poof!"

Mother backed away too, spreading her arms like gates to herd us children back against the kitchen wall.

Fascinated, we kids watched Ivan guide the wheezing, hissing iron over a handkerchief. We could see blue flames through the holes in its sides and smell its gassy alcohol odor.

"My goodness, Margie!" Mother said. "I don't know . . ."

"You'll love it once you get used to it," Marge said. "Come on. Try it."

Cautiously, Mother stepped up to the table and ironed a handkerchief.

"Come on, Dad," Marge said. "Try it."

"Nah." Dad didn't move from his place against the wall. "Your mother will be using it. She'd better get the practice," he said.

My thirteen year old sister, Shirley, the family 'fraidy cat, strode up to the table.

"I'll do it," she said. "I like this thing."

Sure enough, Shirley took control of the iron. She couldn't get enough of it, and she ironed for our whole family until she grew up and left home.

As for the rest of us, we adjusted to the hissing and flaming of the iron. Shirley's reputation for courage and bravery went up a notch in the eyes of her little sisters.

TRIVIA

Questions:

1. What did we call the irons that we heated on the stove?

2. Monday was washday. What day was ironing day?

3. What did housewives use to dampen clothes before they ironed them?

Answers:
1. *Sad irons*
2. *Tuesday*
3. *A sprinkler that fit on the top of a soda bottle*

THE YO-YO MAN
(A city story by Jon)

In today's world, the sight of a strange man loitering in front of the main entrance of a school would be reason to call the police, but in the nineteen forties and fifties, the arrival of the Duncan yo-yo man was a rite of spring.

Word spread fast around the cafeteria: "The yo-yo man's out there!" The high school boys abandoned their lunches. They burst through the school doors into the balmy spring air and gathered around to watch him. The Duncan man was a small guy. He wore a little porkpie hat and a zoot suit. "Duncan Yo-yos" was emblazoned on the back of his light blue jacket. He'd be casually snapping his yo-yos, one in each hand, dancing, and making small talk . . . Sleep, Over-the-Waterfall, Walk-the-Dog, Rock-the-Cradle, Around-the-World, Bite-the-Dog...The yo-yo man didn't stop there. He could put a yo-yo to sleep and stick it in his back pocket, and, when he was ready, he'd yank it out and start it spinning again. He'd put one to sleep and toss it over his shoulder and around the back of his neck, pull it in front of himself, and zing it straight out, so fast, so slick, so perfect.

He had trick yo-yos, some of them five or six inches across, and when he walked the dog, he could send them half way across the street. He had yo-yos with lights, dazzlers, and spinners. Nothing was too bright, too fast, or too gaudy for the little yo-yo man.

When I was in the tenth grade, I thought of him as an older guy; now, I think he was no more than thirty, and already a fast-talking salesman showcasing his wares. We all carried yo-yo's in the spring, so you might wonder what he gained by visiting the school. He had his reasons.

With the crowd gathered around him and the boys producing their yo-yos, the Duncan man started his contest—the prizes for various levels of finesse were always yo-yos in the year's latest colors and designs. By a process of elimination, the competition narrowed to only the best-of-the best, until just the champion was left standing. The grand prize was a special yo-yo, sometimes encrusted with jewels, or lighted, or decorated in a special way. These prize yo yo's couldn't be bought in stores.

Imagine the winner, walking back into the school with his fabulous prize, and a reputation as the man at the top of the North High Yo-yo world!

Of course, the yo-yo man's real purpose in coming to our school was to convince us that the latest yo-yos were better balanced, faster, and slicker than the ones we had, and if we thought we didn't need a new yo-yo, we at least needed special "sleeper string" from the hobby shop, and wax to put on it before we re-strung our yo-yo's.

TRIVIA

Questions:

1. Describe a porkpie hat

2. Yo-Yo's required dexterity and practice to master. Name one other toy or game that required dexterity and practice

3. Name another toy that marked the arrival of spring

Answers:
1. A hat with a flat top and flexible brim
2. Marbles, pick-up sticks, jacks
3. Squirt guns, bean shooters . . .

TO MAKE A BED

For ten years after the depression, my struggling family still clung to its frugal ways. We were do-it-yourselfers of the highest order, not daunted at all by an iron bedstead and a set of open bed springs. All we needed were scraps of cloth to make a quilt, unbleached muslin "sheeting" from Sears Roebuck to make sheets, and straw from the oats after they were threshed to fill mattress ticking.

We'll begin with the mattress.

Every fall after the oat harvest, we reserved a Saturday to work on our mattresses. First, we threw the tired old ones over the upstairs banisters and carried them to the meadow, where we opened them and dumped out last year's straw. Then, we carried the ticking back to the house to be washed. We added sheets, pillowcases, and quilts to the pile near my mother, who stood at the washboard.

Big sisters tended the rinse tub and the wringer, and before noon, the clotheslines sagged under the weight of all that laundry.

While the bedding was drying, we children dusted the bedsprings with a special tapered brush, swept the bedroom floors, washed the windows, and scrubbed the bedsteads.

As soon as the ticking was dry, my sisters and I carried it to the oat field, along with clean shovels and cooking pans, and we scooped in the shimmering straw until the ticking bulged with it. Then Mother came to stitch our mattresses shut with her big needle and sturdy thread.

Probably we were a funny sight, all six of us sisters, boosting those straw ticks into the house, up the stairs, and onto the beds. Still, our work wasn't finished.

Next, we carried in our homemade sheets, the pillows that had been hung out to air, and then the quilts. How beautiful those beds were—so high and puffy, we little sisters had to be lifted into them for the first two nights.

Let's take a minute, though, to peek under the quilt and look at our sheets. Sears offered sheeting, fifteen, thirty, or sixty yards long and three yards wide. Beds were all double size or smaller then, so the thrifty housewife could cut the sheeting to the proper length to fit her beds, then stitch two pieces together to make a sheet seventy-two inches wide. The older sisters spent some time at the treadle sewing machine during the cold winter months, stitching perfect felled seams, making our sheets.

As for the quilts, there were so many beds to cover, Mother made what she called "Scotch quilts", with blocks a foot square, and preferably made of wool. She ordered cotton batting from Sears to fill them, and then she made a backing of big scraps of leftover fabric.

Although I was the youngest and the least able to contribute, I remember the making of our beds as a vigorous, tiring, almost festive part of my childhood.

As the twins and I slipped into clean nighties and settled into our bed on that first night, lying straight and still as paper dolls, I thought the rustle of the straw ticks sounded just like taffeta. The sheets still captured the aroma of the beautiful autumn day, and the freshly laundered quilt with its deep colors was as lovely as a stained glass window. Even a princess couldn't experience more luxury than a small country child snoozing on a straw tick.

TRIVIA

Questions:

1. People in other areas used different mattress stuffing. Name one.

2. Types of fabric were never combined in the same quilt, for example, a cotton quilt was made entirely of cotton, and a wool quilt was made entirely of wool. Why?

3. How was cotton batting packaged?

Answers:

1. Corn husks, cotton . . .

2. When the quilt was washed, mixed fabrics would shrink at different rates

3. In a roll

MAY BASKET

Every spring my mother got a wallpaper catalog in the mail. It was small—maybe eight by ten inches--and it had samples of paper for every room in the house, including the ceilings. Mother took her time looking through the new offerings and turning over each page to see the price of a double or single roll, the color selections, and the "repeat" or "match" which told her how much paper would be wasted when she matched the pattern.

The twins and I hovered around her like vultures, anxiously waiting for her to get to the last page and, if she didn't plan to order any paper, to offer the book to us. We could hardly wait to make off with it.

For my two sisters and me, all of us under ten, that catalog served an important purpose--it supplied our material for May baskets. Never mind that the samples were too small for their intended purpose--we knew how to weave several sheets together, or paste them with a mixture of flour, sugar, and water.

We preferred the flowery bedroom and living room samples, which we combined with dining room stripes and ceiling paper. When we had used all of them, we selected kitchen patterns of teacups, herbs, and quaint, colorful kitchen stoves.

Our baskets were shaky affairs, especially the handles, and they were suitable for holding just a few sprigs of wildflowers. Still, every year, we made plenty of them, and proudly placed them all around the house. To our eyes, they were beautiful.

I didn't know there was another kind of May basket, let alone its connection to unrequited love, until my sister, Shirley, was a teenager. She was a beautiful blond, with a radiant dimpled smile, and a sweet personality. She was so perfect that sometimes I pretended she was Betty Grable.

It didn't occur to me that others might be appreciating Shirley's beauty, too, until one brave young admirer showed his interest with a grand, creative flourish.

Our house was dark and quiet on that first-of-May evening. We were early-rising farmers, for one thing, but we were also constantly strapped for money, and Mother conserved the kerosene for the lamps by sending the family to bed when darkness fell. The twins had snuggled down in their double bed under the quilts. Across the room, in a second double bed, Betty Grable patiently held my hand while I fell asleep because I was afraid of ghosts.

Outside, everything was still, except for the spring night sounds of the peepers and croakers, and an occasional owl. Then, a new sound broke the silence—a car!

We heard it rattling up our dirt road before we saw its headlights flash on the bedroom ceiling.

"Car coming," Bea said, as if the rest of us didn't know.

A car door slammed, and then we heard footsteps in the woodshed, followed by a strong, brisk knock on the kitchen door, and a young man's voice: "May Basket!" This was not a timid fellow.

Shirley lit the lamp, got dressed and hurried downstairs.

Half an hour later, she was back, carrying the lamp in one hand and the most fabulous May Basket we had ever seen in the other. The conical creation was made from shiny pink wrapping paper, its open edge sealed with delicate flowers cut from paper doilies. One small sprig of spring flowers peeked out from its top, but when Shirley lowered it so we could look inside, we could see that the rest of the basket was stuffed with candies.

Shirley casually laid the May Basket on the dresser. "Forever more," she said. "Pretty boy coo."

Nobody knew what that meant. Maybe Shirley didn't even know, but she said it all the time. It could mean anything, from disgust to shock, or even pleasure. We waited for her to tell us.

"That was Charlie Smith," she said. "I don't even like him. Why couldn't it have been Don Fritts, bringing me a May Basket? He's the boy I really like."

She blew out the lamp and climbed back into bed.

"You kids can have the candy in the morning," she told us. Then she took my hand and sighed and said it again:

"Forever more. Pretty boy coo."

TRIVIA

Questions:

1. Name three kinds of penny candy that might have been in the May basket.

2. What was really supposed to happen when a boy hung a May basket on a girl?

3. Charlie Smith drove a doodlebug. What was that?

Answers:
1. Peppermint pillows, caramels, cinnamon buttons . . .
2. She was supposed to chase him and kiss him
3. A jalopy

HORSE MEDICINE

Maybe if our workhorses had been more prone to ailments my father would have been better prepared to doctor them. As it was, his only remedies were a can of turpentine to pour on cuts and a dusty green wine bottle that he kept in the cellar. This would be filled with horse medicine and, with my mother holding the horse's head, shoved down the animal's throat, forcing the poor beast to swallow whatever my father had concocted to put in the bottle.

During the forties farmers way out in the country didn't call the vet; they diagnosed and treated their animals as best they could. Luckily our horses were sturdy and reliable, and never needed to take time off from work because of illness—until Prince, our white horse got sick with what my father thought was a bellyache.

When Dad came in from the barn that night after he had grained the cows, he told us the bad news: "Prince is off his feed." Dad rummaged around in the pantry, looking for something to mix up and put in the wine bottle, but he came out empty-handed.

"One of you kids"—he scanned our faces—"Shirley! Run over to Benton's and see if he's got anything for a horse with the colic. Hurry up, now. Prince is really sick."

Shirley took the shortcut, sprinting across our north meadow, through the woods, down Benton's meadow and straight to his back door.

She returned in twenty minutes, sweating and panting, carrying a newspaper-wrapped bottle along with a note: Mix a tablespoon of this with a quart of water and bring it to a boil, let it cool a little, and pour it down the horse's throat. Don't get this near your eyes. It's hot."

Mother rinsed the green wine bottle, out of respect to the horse, and Dad stirred up the medicine. When it was ready, he poured it in the bottle and my parents raced to the barn.

After they left, the ten-year old twins, and I, who was eight, gathered around the stove. A small amount of the horse medicine was still in the pan.

Bea stirred it thoughtfully. "This smells good," she announced. "Probably it's okay to taste it. After all, who'd give anything poisonous to a horse?"

Bev, ever the cautious one, said, "Don't taste it! Put down the spoon! Whatever it is, it's not meant for people."

"Come over here, Short," Bea said. "Smell it. Doesn't that smell good?" She gave me a little poke with her elbow so I'd know she was tricking Bev.

"Yep. It smells like bubble gum," I said. "Let's taste it."

"Go get a couple of cups," Bea said. "We'll share it."

Bev shoved her way between us. "That's not fair!" she said. "What about me?"

"Well, come on over and take a taste, then," Bea said. And Bev did.

Oh, the yelling! The howling! The screaming! Nobody could do it like Bev.

Dad and Mother were in the house in a flash.

"What happened?" Mother panted. "Who got hurt?"

Bev pointed an accusing finger at Bea and me.

"They made me taste the horse medicine!" she wailed. "My mouth! My tongue! All burned!" Then she yowled some more.

Mother covered Bev's lips and mouth with lard to ease the burning.

Then my parents pulled up two chairs. My mother took me over her knee, and my father took Bea. They spanked us, set us back on our feet, and without a word, raced back to the barn to care for Prince.

When they closed the kitchen door, Bev stopped yowling.

"Blat baby," Bea said.

"Tattletale," I added. "You should have known better than to taste it. Bea and I didn't."

A tiny smile played around Bev's mouth.

"It really did burn a little," she said smugly.

Dad and Mother went to the barn to check on Prince and give him medicine throughout the night, but in the morning our horse was dead.

The next day, my sister Doris returned the bottle of medicine to our neighbor.

"How's the horse?" Benton asked.

"He died," Doris said.

"That's odd," Benton said. "I gave it to my horse, and he died, too."

TRIVIA

Questions:

1. What was the matter with a horse that suffered from heaves?

2. Who hauled away dead horses?

3. If Prince didn't have a bellyache, could he have died from swallowing a nail or piece of wire?

Answers:
1. Asthma or emphysema
2. The rendering company
3. NO! A cow will swallow hardware, but a horse won't

BUZZ SAWS

Yes, we played with buzz saws—humming, spinning blurring-with-speed-buzz saws.

Today, toy makers would cringe at the thought. Oh, the warnings! Oh, the disclaimers!

Warning: This toy requires adult supervision.

Warning: This toy can pinch fingers.

Warning: This toy can tangle in hair.

It doesn't matter--most mothers don't keep button boxes, tins, or jars anymore, and plastic bags or sticky tape have replaced grocery string. There's little chance that a child will construct something as dangerous as a buzz saw.

My sisters and I started making them when we were around six, and we continued to make them until we were about ten.

On cold winter days when we were housebound in the country, those buzz saws served more than one purpose. First, they were fun to make and operate, and second, they gave us younger children some power over our big sisters. (See "Toy can tangle in hair" above.)

Buzz saws are easy to make. Even a six year old can make one with no help. They're more fun, though, if siblings are making them, too.

Here are the instructions:

First, you sort through your mother's collection of buttons, looking for the biggest one you can find with two holes. The bigger the button, the bigger the buzz. If you're the youngest kid, you never get the best button. I know that.

Then you find your family's ball of string, and cut off a length of about three feet. Don't bother to put the ball of string away. A buzz saw's string tends to fray and break quickly.

Feed the string through the holes in the button, and tie the ends in a knot. Now, you have a loop of string with your button in the middle.

Place an index finger in both ends of the loop and twirl the string so it twists the same way a rope swing twists when you twirl around. Now pull the twisted string with your index fingers. Faster! Faster! Hear the button humming--buzz-buzz-buzz. Hear the string—zit-zit-zit, twisting madly in your fingers.

Now, hold your buzz saw as close as you dare to a big sister's ear. Ask if she can hear it humming or if you should get a little closer.

The big sisters made buzz saws, themselves, when they were younger. They know what you're doing.

"I don't want to hear how loud it's humming—just keep away from me with that! If you get that thing any closer and it gets caught in my hair, I'm telling! Now, slow down before you get your fingers pinched."

The faster you pull, the louder your buzz saw buzzes, and the tighter the string twists. The faster you pull, the more ominous it sounds to your big sisters. The faster you pull, the tighter the loops that contain your fingers become. Your fingers are getting pinched, and they're turning purple-red. Owwww!

"Well, stop pulling and let the string untwist, you dope," a big sister says. "I warned you you'd get your fingers pinched."

Who needed a toymaker to warn us?

TRIVIA

Questions:

1. Name two other games that kids played in the forties

2. What was the purpose in playing eeny, meeny, miney mo and one-potato, two potato, three potato, four?

2. Name two games from that era that are still played

Answers:

1. Hide and go seek, Cats Cradle, Musical chairs, Red Light, Green Light . . .

2. To choose sides for games

3. Old Maid, Chinese Checkers, Monopoly . . .

A FAMILY GRADUATION

My sister, Jess, came home from school one May afternoon in 1943 with big news.

"Guess what?" she said as she burst into the kitchen. "I'll be getting a scholarship to CCBI on graduation night."

Mother stopped peeling the potatoes. Dad returned his Uncle Sam plug to the back pocket of his bib overalls.

"What's CCBI?" Dad asked.

"It's a big business school in Syracuse," Jess said.

The ten-year old twins and I, who was eight, stopped what we were doing and stared at Jess.

"Why are you kids staring at me?" Jess said. "Stop it."

"What's a scholarship, Jess?" Bev asked.

"It a kind of wonderful gift," Mother said. "Your sister is going to get it because she worked hard at her school-work, and now she can go somewhere special and learn even more."

"Will it be like the Parker pen and pencil set she won in the essay contest?" I asked.

"Kind of like that," Mother said. "But bigger and more important."

"Well, Jess, you've made us proud," Dad said. He retrieved his Uncle Sam and cut some off with his jackknife.

Mother resumed peeling the potatoes, and the twins and I stood as close as we dared to Jess, just to share her excitement.

Jess's Parker pen and pencil set had come wrapped in gold paper and tied with a white ribbon. Probably the scholarship would be in a bigger box. I couldn't even imagine how it would be wrapped. I couldn't wait for graduation.

In early June, Mother and the big sisters began preparations for the grand occasion. This would be a three-evening event, and there was plenty to do. Dad's white shirt was freshly washed, dipped in the bluing, then in the starch, and dried in the sun. Then the lace collar that attached to Mother's good black dress followed Dad's shirt. During that busy time, somebody was always standing at the ironing board. Our best dresses were washed, starched, and ironed, shoes were polished, and finally, on the afternoon of the big evening, Mother heated water for baths and shampoos.

Finally, we were ready to go--Dad and Mom, my five sisters, and me.

Our car was an oldie—a little yellow Ford with a rumble seat and a tattered ragtop, stuck in the down position. Into this vehicle—the most compact of compacts--the eight members of my family found spaces for themselves. Doris, Jess, and Shirley squeezed into the rumble seat and slid their skirts up so the twins could perch on their knees. I rode on my mother's lap in the front. After he cranked the car over, Dad, resplendent in his white shirt and black suit, climbed into the driver's seat.

We rattled down our dirt road, and then turned onto the paved county highway.

White painted houses and red barns stood like official greeters along the way. The fields smelled of fresh cut hay, and cows grazed in the pastures. What a perfect night for our grand outing!

When we arrived at the cemetery Dad turned the car in and parked it next to the family plot.

"I don't dare drive it into town because it's not licensed," he explained. "We'll just walk down the road 'til we get to the sidewalks. It's only a quarter of a mile."

Mother said, "Your father will go ahead, and then a big sister, and a little sister, and a big sister, and a little sister, and another big sister, and a little sister, and I'll come last. Stay way over on the side of the road in case a car comes."

Dad had some advice to add:

"Probably you'll see people sitting on their porches. I don't want you staring. Just watch where you're going."

We walked out of the cemetery and onto the road.

I thought we looked wonderful.

When we came to the sidewalk, we broke rank and clustered together until we got to the school. Usually the auditorium smelled like dusty curtains, wax from the stage, and leather seats, but tonight it smelled like sweaty backs, aftershave and perfume, and stale tobacco smoke. The grown-ups had taken over.

The first night of graduation was always a Sunday, and a minister in a black robe and dark-rimmed glasses spoke to the graduates and their families.

I patted my mother's arm.

"He looks like an owl, doesn't he?" I whispered.

"Shhh. Be still. I'm listening," she said.

I saw Jess on the stage in her cap and gown and I waved to her, but she didn't see me.

The auditorium was hot and stuffy, and the minister talked and talked.

There'd be no scholarship for Jess tonight. I slumped against my father and went to sleep.

Monday night was class night. The graduates gave each other little gifts, and everybody laughed. I didn't get the jokes. Again I leaned against Dad and went to sleep.

The third night, it happened.

Our principal stepped onto the stage and handed out the diplomas.

"Listen now," Mother said. "She'll be getting her scholarship any minute."

"Jessie Rose Martin," the principal said. "A full scholarship to CCBI. Congratulations, Jessie."

He handed Jess a piece of paper.

I couldn't believe it. All she got was a piece of paper. No gold wrapping, no beautiful bow. The principal handed out more awards and congratulated all the graduates. Then, the band began to play and the somber, black-robed participants filed up the center aisle of the auditorium. Graduation was over.

We walked back up the hill to the cemetery. The evening had turned cooler, and the seats of our car were wet with dew. We all climbed in and dad cranked the car over, got in the driver's seat and took us home.

Mother fumbled for matches and lit the lamp.

"Goodness," she said. "It's nine-thirty. You children go right to bed."

After all the excitement of the last three nights, we really were exhausted.

As far as the scholarship, Jess never used it.

Syracuse was a big city, and Jess was a country girl. She wouldn't know what to do there, or how to behave. Besides, the bus fare would cost nearly fifty cents a day. How could our family afford that?

So the scholarship turned out to be just what I thought it was--a piece of paper. Still, it had been something to be proud of, and I was happy for us all.

TRIVIA

Questions:

1. What was the name given to the Sunday night service when the minister spoke?

2. The graduates marched into the auditorium to music. What was it called?

3. They marched back out to different music. What was it called?

Answers:

1. Baccalaureate

2. Processional ("Pomp and Circumstance")

3. Recessional

FREEBIES

During World War II, it seemed as if everything was rationed--meat, sugar, coffee, shoes, nylon stockings, gasoline, rubber, butter, and candy (of course).

Imagine the elementary school children's delight when, after the war, we were treated to an unexpected variety of giveaways. The food, I'm sure, was from Uncle Sam--tiny paper cups with two dried apricots that the cafeteria ladies doled out in the middle of the afternoon. Then we switched to prunes. A few weeks after that, we lined up for two-inch high paper cups with about three tablespoons of carefully measured orange juice.

We elementary kids loved walking to the end of the hall, lining up at a table, and devouring our little treats, dropping the paper cups in the wastebasket, and walking back to our classrooms. I thought we were enjoying tiny, impromptu tea parties.

Things got better.

A small bar of pink Lifebuoy soap appeared on my school desk now and then. It smelled like medicine, and I never opened it, but I was so delighted that somebody had given me a present, I gave it a special place on my dresser.

Little bars of Ivory appeared, too. They smelled clean and fresh, and I tucked them in my underwear drawer as a substitute sachet.

Then, smooth, golden wood rulers arrived. "Do Unto Others As You Would Have Them Do Unto You" marched in stern letters along the bottom of the front, and on the back, in fine script were the words "Coca-Cola". They were real keepers!

The Red Cross pins weren't free and they weren't really keepers, but for a day or two they were high fashion in second grade. These stylish little items were made from thin white metal embellished with a red cross. The teacher kept them in a box on her desk, and kids could buy one for as little as a penny. They were easy to wear--just bend a little tab over and put it on your shirt. In a few days the novelty wore off, and we went from everybody wearing a pin to nobody wearing a pin. Second graders are fickle.

Sometimes we got paper book covers and occasionally, bookmarks. I don't know who bestowed these luxuries upon us, but I, for one, was delighted. We had been through a war, and, even though we were just kids, we had sacrificed, too.

We deserved those freebies.

The following September I moved into third grade, and my cheery little life went straight downhill.

My teacher's name was Miss Roche. Her complexion was pale gray, and her body looked hard and bony beneath her stern, colorless clothes. I could tell she had a cold heart, too. The French word for "rock" is "Roche" Her name was perfect.

Worst of all, I was sure Miss Roche didn't care about me.

Then I discovered the government didn't care about me anymore, either. No more bright orange apricots, purple prunes and watery yellow orange juice. Uncle Sam offered me something else. One day, Miss Roche, walking backward in her brown loafers, led us down to the nurse's office to be weighed. This was a surprising development, because we generally were weighed when the doctor came to give us physicals.

"Teeth and tonsils," he'd announce. "Teeth and tonsils."

The nurse would write that down. Practically everybody had teeth and tonsils, but not much else that interested our school doctor.

Our little trip to the nurse's office with Miss Roche changed that.

I, along with about five of my classmates, was given a new diagnosis—"underweight"--but Uncle Sam and the school cafeteria knew how to cure our problem.

The next day, Miss Roche separated us from our friends and placed us at the end of the cafeteria table.

I looked at the other kids--all of them dirty and not very bright. There I was, an honor roll student and, thanks to my mother's washboard, as clean as anybody.

Still, there was hope.

I had never tasted our cafeteria lunches. They looked delicious, served on white china plates decorated with thin orange and black stripes (the school colors) and laden with fragrant meat, mashed potatoes, a vegetable, a little bottle of milk, and a small cardboard cup of ice cream, complete with a flat wooden spoon.

I'd gladly tolerate the new seating arrangement in exchange for a "Special Plate".

That first day, a cafeteria lady arrived with a tray holding five of the beautiful school cups. When she put them down I saw that they contained watery pink-tinged hot cocoa, topped with scum.

The other kids practically lapped it up. I couldn't drink it. I absolutely couldn't.

Miss Roche stood behind me.

"Drink that delicious cocoa," she said. "I'm right here watching to be sure you do."

I drank the cocoa.

The next day the cafeteria lady came with a tray of five lovely bowls. They were filled with curdled tomato soup.

I absolutely, positively couldn't eat it.

From the corner of my eye, I saw Miss Roche's loafers moving behind me.

"Come on," she said. "Eat that lovely soup. The other children have already finished theirs, and cafeteria time is almost up."

She turned to check on the students at the other end of the table, and I poured the curdled mess into my lunch box. I quickly realized I had made a mistake. The soup began to seep out of the slots on each end of my blue domed lunch container.

There was nothing I could do. I dripped a path of soup back to my room, and down the aisle to the coat closet, where the soup puddled all afternoon.

It still wasn't finished. At dismissal, it dripped on my boot, and then onto the bus.

I couldn't wait to get home and tell my mother.

She dumped out the remainder of the mess and rinsed my lunch box.

Then she wrote a note to Miss Roche and sealed it in an envelope. She didn't tell me what she had written.

The next day at lunchtime, Miss Roche grasped me firmly by the arm.

"You can go back and sit with your friends," she said. Her lips were tight and unsmiling.

I was grinning like a 'possum.

TRIVIA

Questions:

Speaking of free:

1. Name one free prize that was tucked in cereal boxes in the 1940's.

2. What special prize separated the layers of shredded wheat?

3. What prize was included in laundry detergent?

Answers:

1. Sheriff badges, decoder rings, toy wristwatches

2. Thin balsa wood airplane patterns that could be cut out and assembled

3. Dinnerware. It was also available at gas stations

THE HAY WAGON

When I was still too young to read, I spent a fair amount of time leafing through my mother's old postcard album. Some of the cards showed lovely ladies wearing ornate hats and dresses, others were pictures of buildings, and others, I thought, were probably funny, if a person were old enough to understand a joke.

My favorite, and most puzzling, postcard showed young farmers in straw hats, loading a hay wagon. Ladies stood in the hay field in their long summer dresses, watching the young men, and everybody in the picture was smiling. How could that be? When our family was putting in hay, nobody smiled. My big sisters wore old slacks and shirts. My father wore his usual blue work shirt, bib overalls, and striped railroad-style cap. At our farm, there was no glamour and no joy in the hayfield.

When I was old enough to help, sometimes I thought about that picture. It annoyed me, not because of what it showed, but what it didn't.

After our hay loader broke, my father loaded hay onto the wagon with a pitchfork. The job he assigned to my sisters and me was to stomp it down by climbing onto the wagon and walking around on the hay to compact it so Dad could get a good big load.

When I thought about that picture, I realized that their wagon had side rails, or racks, that contained the hay and kept the hapless hay stompers from sliding off onto the ground. Our wagon didn't have racks. When it was piled high with slippery hay, we tried to keep away from the sides. Falling off would be no laughing matter.

Along with the possibility of a quick slide to the ground, we dealt with unexpected visitors that rode up on Dad's pitchfork. They were nowhere to be seen on that post-card. Sometimes we got a nest of mice. Other times a snake joined us. We'd get a glimpse of the mice and snakes before they burrowed into the hay and laid low until they were swooped up into the haymow on the big hayfork, where they could take up housekeeping or somehow escape.

The ground bees were another story. When they land-ed on the wagon, they didn't disappear into the hay. Heck no! They attacked in a mad fury, swarming around our fac-es, getting caught in our hair, and buzzing angrily down our shirts. They terrified me.

I was on the wagon with my big sister, Shirley, one day when a nest of bees arrived. We were easy targets, high up on a big load of hay, and confined to the center of the wagon.

I struggled through the hay, heading straight toward my big sister.

Shirley was calm. "Stand still, Short," she said quietly. "They'll go away in a minute."

I couldn't do it. I covered my face with my arms and screamed for Dad--and then I dove for cover--right under Shirley's baggy blue sweater.

Shirley wasn't calm and quiet any more.

"Get out of there!" she yelled.

Poor Shirley high stepped back and forth and round and round, fighting to keep her place in the middle of the wagon, and at the same time, struggling to keep her balance.

"Now they're really coming after me!" Shirley said. "Get out! Get out!"

I couldn't. I joined her in her mad dance, burrowing frantically under her sweater, and stretching it down over myself with both hands.

I heard Dad climb up on the wagon and I knew, from the swish swish of his cap he was swatting the bees away.

"They're gone, Short," he said. "What's the matter with you, scared of a few bees."

I inched my way out from Shirley's sweater. Dad jerked his chin to one side to let me know what he thought of a wimp like me. Then he climbed back down and started forking up the hay again.

As for Shirley, she's in her seventies now, but she still remembers that incident on the hay wagon.

Even today, I think, if a photographer tried to take a picture of her working at haying, posing for a cheery postcard, he'd have a tough time making her smile.

TRIVIA

Questions:

1. Name another method of harvesting hay

2. What can happen if hay is wet when it is put in the barn?

3. What crop is commonly stored in silos?

Answers:

1. Baling

2. It can create spontaneous combustion and set the barn on fire

3. Corn

BICYCLE RINGELIVIA
(A city story by Jon)

Maybe you have never heard of Bicycle Ringelivia. Maybe the guys in my neighborhood made it up. I'm not even sure of the spelling.

If you were a ten or twelve year old boy in the forties, before bicycle helmets were mandatory, and before kids were introduced to the perils of bike riding by hovering parents, maybe you played a similar game.

Bicycle Ringelivia was played after dark on summer nights, when the back and side yards of the neighborhood were slippery with dew and littered with hazards—fenced yards with gates, coiled hoses, Mrs. Gray's goldfish pond, clotheslines, hammocks, little kids' toys--all the trappings of summer lay waiting to dismount a sweaty, madly peddling kid playing ringelivia.

These were the rules:

First, we designated a jail. The sidewalk in front of Don Ross's house was perfect, because it was centrally located within the three-block area where we played. Besides, Don sneaked his dad's bottle of anisette outside, and we all had a little nip before the game began. I didn't care for the taste of the stuff, but because it was grown-up and forbidden, I sampled it every time it was offered.

We chose sides, and one team rode off to hide, vanishing over the riverbank, lurking behind the neighbors' hedges, and quietly melting into dark driveways. After a short wait, the other team rode out to find them. This sounds like an ordinary game of hide-and-seek, but to young boys with galloping imaginations, the pursued kids could almost feel the hot breath of a posse breathing down their necks. The pursuers were as stern and relentless as any sheriff and his men.

When a guy got caught he was hustled off to jail, and he remained there, guarded by a jailer, of course, until all of his team was rounded up. His only hope was that somebody from his team would blaze through the jail, ducking and weaving to avoid being tagged by the guard. This was no easy task, since the jail was only the width of the sidewalk, and about twenty feet long. A successful run through the jail, however, resulted in the release of all the prisoners.

By some miracle, apart from the usual arguments over who really sneaked in, and who really got tagged, this game generally went smoothly, and despite the hazards that lurked in the dark, the players went home, exhausted, sweaty, and happy, and without a scratch when the game was over.

Then, my friend Bubby tangled with Mrs. Burt's clothesline. Bubby, a tall, skinny kid, was part of the posse that night, and I was one of the pursued. He was right behind me, riding furiously. I was pedaling for all I was worth, gauging my speed to jump off our stone wall and barrel toward Don's house to rescue my friends from their prison.

I turned to check on my pursuer just in time to see Bubby flip backward off his bike and land with a thud in Mrs. Burt's back yard. The clothesline had caught him right in the neck. Bubby's red, balloon-tired bike sped on without him, until it finally wobbled and crashed.

Bubby lay on his back in the lawn for a few minutes. Then he cautiously got to his feet, and before I could even ask if he was okay, he jumped back on his bike and came after me.

That night, nobody noticed that Bub couldn't talk, but when the game was over and everybody went home, we didn't see him again for three days.

We boys discussed Bub's encounter with the clothesline for a week, and even the guys that didn't see it described what they saw.

"…And he just jumped right back on," we marveled. "No moaning or groaning. No going home so his mom could check him for broken bones—nope. Not Bubby. He just jumped right back on! What a guy!"

We shortened his name to "Bub".

TRIVIA

Questions:

1. Name two brands of bikes from that era.

2. Not all bikes had chain guards. How did kids solve that problem?

3. Girls could add attachments to their bikes. Name one.

Answers:

1. Raleigh, Shelby, Columbia, Western Flyer

2. They rolled up their pant leg

3. Baskets, bells, streamers

EVERYTHING BUT THE WAR
(A city story by Jon)

Our small city was well supplied with stores. Whether you needed hardware, shoes, furniture, jewelry, a musical instrument, fresh roasted nuts, or an elegant fur coat, you could go to downtown Binghamton, NY and fulfill your heart's desire. Eye catching window displays invited shoppers inside, where merchandise was carefully arranged to encourage shoppers to open their purses and wallets.

The Army Surplus Store, however, marched to its own drum when it displayed its wares. Inside its dim musty interior, the odor of Cosmoline, the petroleum-based waxy substance that coated all things metal, hung in the air like a manly perfume. 2' x 2' x 3' bins cluttered the floor. They were filled to overflowing with everything from flashlights equipped with compasses, half-shelters, hand operated fire extinguishers and air raid sirens, ammunition, skis, military-style clothing, bayonets and knives, rifles, canteens, and trench shovels with folding handles. The Army surplus store sold practically everything to do with war except the war itself.

The people who frequented that establishment didn't care about lovely window displays and artful in-store arrangements--they shopped there for the bargain prices and the ever-changing selection. It was a guy store, and that included teenage boys like my friends and me.

We'd have loved to have taken armloads of everything, but, even though the prices at the Army Surplus Store were rock bottom, we couldn't afford to buy much. The summer that I was fifteen, my friends and I decided to buy half-shelters. These small, floorless tents could be fastened together to accommodate two people. Even today they are popular with scout troops. The surplus store carried sleeping bags, but they were beyond our means. We settled for blankets and pillows from home.

Almost overnight, tents sprouted like mushrooms in Bub Burley's back yard. Even Bub, who could have slept in his own bed, moved into a half-shelter with a buddy. In those cramped, uncomfortable nighttime quarters, we hatched a plan for a major summer construction project behind Bub's garage. Creative geniuses that we were, we decided to make our own miniature golf course.

I have recently learned that miniature golf, as we know it actually originated in my hometown of Binghamton, NY. In the late 1930's Joe and Bob Taylor began building and operating their own miniature golf courses. By the late 1950's, the Taylors were mass-producing waterwheels, castles, and windmills, and most miniature golf supply catalogues carried those Taylor obstacles.

I have also been told that portable courses were enjoyed by our military during certain wars, but I'm pretty sure none of them made their way to our local Army surplus store.

My friends and I knew only two things about the game: We loved to play. Playing cost money, and we were always strapped for cash.

We collected raw materials—discarded lumber from Bub's uncle's sawmill, soup cans, an old tire, a few old golf clubs and balls from various garages, and some simple tools. Then we agreed on a site—a fifteen by twenty foot stretch of land behind Bub's garage. In that tight little space, we laid out four holes.

Things got off to a rough start when we tried to saw our free lumber. It was so hard, we all had to take turns with the saw. By the time we managed to cut those boards to the proper length we were convinced that we had been given ironwood. Some of us, including Bub, believe that to this day.

The soup-can holes we designed were really pretty good.

One hole was a straight shot into an old tire, cut and looped so the ball would go in one side and come out heading for the hole. We had to whack the ball pretty hard to get it to go up and over inside the tire, but if we whacked it too hard, it sailed straight over the "hole".

Another was a mound of dirt with the hole in the top of the mound. If we had been professionals, we'd have chosen a specific club for that hole, but we were rank amateurs, with a smattering of old irons to work with, and we just whaled away until the ball got up the mound, and sometimes over it, without stopping.

Another hole had two mounds of dirt in front of it, and again, the trick was to hit the ball just hard enough to get it over the mounds, but not so hard it flew past the hole.

Our fourth creation was a zigzag with two angles to get to the hole. We had to zap the ball to bank it off the angles. Like the other holes, this one required just the right combination of strength and restraint.

Blame it on our poor and limited equipment, or our young ages (more strength than restraint) or bad course design, but conquering that golf course occupied us for the good part of a summer.

Fifty years later, Bub paid a visit to his childhood home. He walked around behind the garage to see if anything was left of our grand construction project. The mounds and holes were gone, and the wood had rotted away, but Bub could still see the faint indentations of our golf course.

TRIVIA

Questions:

1. What is the record score for an eighteen-hole Minigolf game?

2. Why is Minigolf sometimes called "Putt-Putt"?

3. During two different wars, the U.S. Government contracted with a minigolf company to manufacture pre-fabricated minigolf courses to be shipped to our servicemen overseas. Which wars were they?

Answers:
1. Eighteen
2. It's named for the putter used in regular golf
3. The Korean and Viet Nam wars

POLIO!
(A city story by Jon)

I was seven years old in 1942. My older brother had joined the Marine Corps that year, and my parents didn't know where he was, or even if he was alive. Like many families, mine sat glued to the radio night after night, my father in a haze of cigarette smoke in his Morris chair, my mother sitting across from him, making tiny stitches on a red and white quilt.

I was expected to keep quiet until they had finished listening to every last word of war news.

That summer, two friends, each who lived within three houses of mine, were diagnosed with polio and were whisked off to a special hospital, sixty miles away. My parents knew about polio, but they didn't expect it to come to our neighborhood. They didn't know why it had attacked those two youngsters, or what had caused it, or how to protect their own precious child.

Now, my parents were worried about both my brother and me.

They listened to the news about the war, and then they listened for news about new polio cases.

I didn't share in their worries. I was a wiggly seven-year old with my own concerns: School would be starting in a few weeks, and I didn't want to go. I had just learned to swim, and the bathhouses along the river had been closed all summer because of the polio scare. We were eating fish practically every night because of the meat rationing, and I wasn't all that fond of fish. Oh, the woes of a seven-year old.

I don't remember why we were in the car that August Saturday, but I recall every other detail of that afternoon.

We were driving along Main Street, the busiest thoroughfare in Binghamton, NY. We were passing the Montgomery Ward store.

I can only guess at how I was behaving—a bored seven-year-old in need of attention, probably bouncing around behind my father, kicking the back of his seat, complaining that I was thirsty, whining that I was hungry, fretting that the prickly upholstery on our '36 Plymouth was making my bare legs itch.

My parents, busy with their own thoughts, didn't respond.

Seven-year-old boys don't give up. I suspect that I kicked harder, complained louder, and whined and fretted some more.

My father just kept driving. My mother didn't bother to turn around

I tried a new approach.

"I hope I get polio," I said.

Well! My father screeched the car to a halt right in the middle of the street. He yanked me out of the back seat, and planted solid, stinging spanks on my bottom, right in front of the other drivers and all the people on the sidewalk.

"Don't you ever say that!" he said grimly. "Don't you ever say that again!"

He shoved me back into the car, got behind the wheel, and drove home.

I had never been spanked before. I don't think my father had even scolded me until that day. Long after the sting of his hand had subsided, I smarted from the embarrassment of it all. I couldn't understand why my father had turned on me for merely saying five little words.

New medical terms crept into our vocabulary--paralysis, iron lungs, and braces. Even older children feared polio. It was, after all, mostly a children's disease. Still, I was too young to make the connection between my friends and those new, scary words. We weren't talking about them were we?

More than a year passed before my friends came home from the polio hospital. The neighbors closed a side street to traffic and organized a party to welcome them back.

The boys stayed close to their parents, cautiously surveying their old neighbors. I was shocked to see they'd been fitted with leg braces, and they used crutches to get around. They weren't carefree, wiggly kids anymore. They seemed somber and determined, and more grown up than the rest of us.

Over the years, I understood that the two of them had been through a war as terrible as any war, torn from their families, and placed in a hospital that must have been a living nightmare. Parents came when they could, but sixty miles was a long way, driving over the two-lane roads of that era, and the parents had jobs and other children to care for. Many didn't own cars, and they relied on the generosity of others or took the bus to visit their sick children. Still, mostly the polio victims faced their battles alone.

Eventually, my friends were able to walk without crutches, ride their bikes again, play sports, and slip back into the mainstream of the neighborhood.

They grew into tough, motivated men, with good careers and stable families. Maybe their childhood experience with polio was a contributing factor in their success.

TRIVIA

Questions:

1. Who developed the first vaccine for polio?

2. Who developed the vaccine that could be given on a sugar cube?

3. When polio victims suffered from such severe paralysis they couldn't breathe, they were placed in a special device that breathed for them. What was it called?

Answers:

1. Jonas Salk

2. Albert Sabin

3. An iron lung

WHEN THE CLOCK STOPPED

Our alarm clock, the only timepiece my family owned, ticked away its days on a shelf in the kitchen. At night, before my father crawled into bed, he retrieved the Westclox from its daytime perch, wound both the clock and the alarm, and pulled out the little button that would start it clattering at five-thirty the following morning. He put it on his dresser where it ticked away its nights.

This ritual, always performed in his sock feet, usually inspired my father to hum, maybe because it wasn't his job to respond to its insistent racket the following morning. It wasn't his job to start the fire in the kitchen stove, or make his breakfast before he went to the barn, or rouse my sisters and me in time to get ready for school. My mother and the clock kept order in our family's life.

There would come a time, though, when the clock fell down on the job. At first, my parents refused to believe their reliable old friend was failing them. Maybe Dad hadn't wound it tightly enough. He'd give its key an extra twist. Maybe he had wound it too tightly. He'd give it a hearty shake. Sometimes these tactics worked for a while and the clock resumed ticking as if nothing had happened.

Actually, something big had happened. The clock was no longer trustworthy, and in a short time, it let us down again We weren't sure how long it had been stopped before we noticed, and we lost our sense of time.

Since we had no radio or telephone, our only solution was to run up through the orchard to the point on our farm that was closest to the town four miles away and listen for the noon whistle. When we heard it, we raced back to the kitchen with the news, and Dad shook the clock and wound it, and if we were lucky, our precious timepiece resumed its duties.

That idea only worked if the clock stopped on a summer day, when we could guess from the position of the sun when the noon whistle would blow so we could be ready. During the dark days of winter when we couldn't depend on the sun to give us a hint, and the snow was too deep to run through the orchard anyway, and especially if the clock stopped sometime in the night, my mother flew into a panic. She'd rush to the stairs in the morning, calling as she came,

"Girls! Girls! Get up! The clock stopped! Hurry, now! You don't want to miss the bus!"

We'd leap out of bed and get dressed. Never mind breakfast—with coats unbuttoned and hats and mittens in our hands, we flew out the door and down our quarter-mile hill to the bus stop.

Sometimes the bus would be waiting. More often, we were the ones who'd be waiting, marching up and down the road to keep our feet warm and grumbling that mom must have woke up right on time, even without the alarm, and we had raced to the bus stop at least an hour early.

That night when we got off the bus we'd ask our driver for the time, and we'd fly up the hill to tell our parents. We estimated the time it had taken to run up the hill and set the clock accordingly. Give or take five minutes, we were marching (however temporarily) along with the rest of the world. We all suspected that our trustworthy clock wasn't to be trusted any more.

When our faithful timepiece gave its absolute final effort my father bought another—same brand, same features (an alarm), and same color—a white clock with a white face and black numerals and hands.

Mother put it on the shelf in the kitchen, and dad wound it (humming) at night, and mother and the reliable new clock brought order back into our lives.

TRIVIA

Questions:

1. Name two other types of clocks that were common before electricity

2. Name one famous clock anywhere in the world

3. Name one other source for setting that clock

Answers:

1. Mantle clock, Grandfather clock, Cockoo clock

2. Big Ben, Doomsday clock, The atomic clock in Colorado

3. Church bells, factory whistles . . .

GLAMOUR GIRLS

I was in the eighth grade when I realized I needed to get moving in the world of glamour.

Our homemaking teacher had decided that we girls (there were only girls in home ec.) would sew makeup capes. These were pieces of fabric cut in a circle, with a slit down the front and ties at the neck.

My mother sorted through her collection of cotton and selected a piece of green material, which she was careful to inform me was "a lovely hunter green". It was ugly. Nevertheless, I slipped it in a brown grocery bag and trudged off to school.

The teacher was bubbling with enthusiasm. How handy our capes would be when we applied our makeup! No more spilled powder, rouge, or lipstick! No more hair that escaped from our brush! When our date arrived, we'd look perfect!

Whoa! I had no powder, rouge, or lipstick. At thirteen, I hadn't even entertained the notion of a date. I did own a hairbrush, but my hair stayed on my head securely enough to suit me. What was I going to do with a makeup cape?

I began to notice the other girls in my class. Although I never asked them, I suspected that they, too, were wondering why they needed makeup capes. Their faces looked as clean and shiny as mine, with the exception of a smear of very light, almost self-conscious lipstick here and there.

The teacher had made her point. I should at least be paying attention to whatever it was that I needed to achieve glamour.

I took an inventory of my teenaged sister's dresser. Arranged carefully on a hand-embroidered dresser scarf, were all the glamour items that she owned: Combs, brushes, Apple Blossom dusting powder, Ipana toothpaste (Brusha, brusha, brusha/ Get the new Ipana/With the brand-new flavor/ It's dandy for your teeth) and Teel tooth liquid (Beauty in every drop) Ponds cold cream (She's engaged/ She's lovely/ She Uses Ponds), metal hair curlers, wave clips, plenty of bobby pins, an empty Evening in Paris perfume bottle, leg makeup, Tangee lipstick, orange wood sticks, nail files, Jergens Lotion, Amami wave set, bright bottles of nail polish, arranged in a "V", and remover. There were also tissues and rods from a Toni Home Permanent. (Which twin has the Toni?)

I had amassed a little over a dollar, garnered from searching under my father's car seats and behind the sofa cushions, picking blackberries for a neighbor, and gathering a little change at Christmas. With hands behind my back, because I wasn't allowed to touch my sister's possessions, I inhaled the delicious smells of her glamour--the almond scent of the Jergens, the clean aroma of the Ponds, the wintergreen tang of the toothpaste, and the almost imperceptible contribution of the Apple Blossom. Then, I considered my options.

My older sister was generous with her toothpaste, dripping a small amount of Teel on my brush, or squeezing on a dab of Ipana. No sense in buying that. Her dusting powder was free for the asking. I didn't feel any need for Ponds, and the idea of sleeping on metal curlers was too much for me. I narrowed my decision to Tangee lipstick--that half-embarrassed smear of very pale lip coloring that some of the other girls were wearing. I would join the ranks.

When my sewing session in homemaking class was over, I brought my makeup cape home, folded it carefully, and placed it in the bottom of the ragbag. I wish I had asked my classmates what they did with theirs.

TRIVIA

Questions:

1. Why did my sister arrange her bottles of nail polish in a "V"?

2. Who sang the Ipana jingle?

3. What was wave set?

Answers:

1. "V" for Victory! The war was on!

2. Bucky Beaver

3. Thick goo that women combed through their hair before setting on rollers or pin curls

CIRCUS WORKER
(A city story by Jon)

Today, circus visitors walk into an arena or a stadium of some kind, buy their tickets, and settle into their seats someplace up in the stratosphere. They can't smell the elephants or the bears, they can't see the sweaty faces of the trapeze artists, and they can't appreciate what goes on behind the scenes to set up the circus. Years ago, a teenage boy could learn first hand about erecting the big top, and if all went well, he could walk right in and see the show for free. If all went well.

The circus train barely made it into the freight yards in Binghamton, New York when word began to spread among the guys: "Get down there. Tell them you want to help. Ask them what they'll pay."

On the Friday afternoon of its arrival, a half dozen of my friends and I hurried down to the circus train where it was stopped on a siding. As we walked past the cars, we could see the lions, bears, elephants, tigers, and horses in their railroad car cages. That mini tour was a preview of things to come. I could hardly wait to go!

We wandered around until we found a man who seemed to be in charge and we, along with a dozen or so other guys, offered our services.

"Be here at six tomorrow," the man told us. "When you're done, I'll give you all free passes to the circus. How's that?"

We looked at each other and grinned. What a deal!

The next morning when the fog still hung heavy over our river valley, my friend, Danny, and I, two skinny four-teen year olds, hustled down to lend a hand.

Nobody asked us if we had hernias, bad hearts, bad knees, or other physical failings. Nobody even asked our names. Pressing work was waiting to be done, and we had hired on to do it. By the end of that day, Danny and I had all the circus experience we needed to last our lifetimes, and we'd earned those free passes a hundred times over.

The circus workers had laid out the exact location of the big top on an ample stretch of flat land not far from the tracks. Our job would be to carry about a hundred long, cumbersome tent poles with metal pins on their ends, place them in the grommets in the tent, and little by little, boost up the big top. The poles were heavy, the tent was heavy, and the circus workers were unrelenting. "Get that pole in the hole! Come on, come on!"

We ran. We grabbed poles, stuffed their pins in the grommets, boosted up the tent, and ran again for another pole. There'd be a matinee that afternoon, and the pressure was on.

The morning fog burned away by nine o'clock, and we were treated to a boiling sun glaring down on a sultry, windless day. With tee shirts sticking to our backs and sweat dripping in our eyes, we kept up our pace. Nobody suggested a rest or a drink. "Move it. Move it!"

Finally, somebody panted, "Hey, we're almost done. Look, there's our first pole."

We struggled to the end. I couldn't wait for a rest and at least a gallon of some wet, cold drink. Anything would do.

"There's the frames for the bleachers," the man said. "Get them in the tent and put them together."

We carried in the frames while some other guys raced in with the boards that formed the seats, and the circus workers, waiting to complete the job, started hollering again: "Move it! Come on! Move it!"

The church bells were tolling twelve o'clock when we finished with the bleachers. A man stepped inside the tent, gave us each a hotdog and a soda, and handed out our free passes for the afternoon matinee. The circus was finished with us.

Danny and I trudged home.

I drank a whole pitcher of iced tea, took a cool bath and changed into fresh clothes. Then I headed for the sun porch and stretched out on the glider for a half-hour's rest before I walked down to see the circus. The house was quiet. A cool breeze wafted through the screens.

I woke up at four-thirty, just when the matinee was ending. My free pass had expired. Danny swears to this day that he was given a bad hot dog. He spent the afternoon recovering from an awful bellyache, and his free pass expired, too.

TRIVIA

Questions:

1. What are circus workers called?

2. Smaller tents surrounded the big top. What were the shows in the smaller tents called?

3. Somebody stood outside the smaller tents and tried to lure people inside. What were they called?

Genius question ***
Who was the most famous clown ever?

Answers:
1. Roustabouts
2. Sideshows
3. Barkers
Emmet Kelly

ELDERBERRY TATTOOS

In the nineteen forties, when I was a farm kid, we canned every wild berry we could find. Starting with the strawberries in June, we progressed to blackberries in August, and in early September, we picked the dreaded elderberries that drooped over our dirt road. They were tiny, squishy berries filled with purple juice, and although we could quickly strip them from their thin branches, it took forever to fill a pan. Never mind bringing a pail for elderberries—we'd have never filled it. The other problem with elderberries was that my father was the only one who ate those pies. If the whole family had liked them, and if we could have feasted on their juicy goodness as we picked, the way we did with the other berries, we might have felt better about our assignment, but the twins and I hated the taste of them. Besides, they were always covered with road dust.

The early September weather was hot and humid when we picked the elderberries, and the road was dusty, and that made our mouths feel fuzzy, and grasshoppers were at their irritating unpredictable worst, springing up from the sides of the road to light on our sweaty legs. There were a hundred reasons to grumble about our sad lot, out there picking those darn berries.

I suppose it didn't help that our attention spans weren't very long—the twins were around twelve, and I was nine—but we lost interest in our job in practically no time at all.

We sat down in the grass along the road, shaded from the sun by the elderberry bushes, and dolefully compared the contents of our pans to see how many we had managed to pick.

Then Bev took a few berries from her pan and, pressing them along her leg, she made a tattoo—"B.A.M." Beverly Ann Martin. Bea and I wrote our initials on our legs, too. Bev made a heart around her initials and wrote "B.A.M. + R.O.S." She didn't really have a boyfriend; she just chose some random initials. Bea and I tried it, too. If we hadn't been sitting down, we might have fallen down from laughing. We drew stripes around our legs and made tic-tac-toe squares and big watches on our arms.

We were so eager to share our cleverness with our mother we finished picking the berries in record time and hurried back to the house. We thought our mother would laugh. She didn't.

"Oh, my!" she said, wrinkling her forehead in disapproval. "School starts the day after tomorrow, and nothing stains like elderberries. How did you think you'd get that writing off yourselves?"

Suddenly, there was nothing humorous about our tattoos.

Bea filled the wash dish with clean water. We lathered ourselves with soap and scrubbed, but our tattoos stayed put. We tried Fels Naptha laundry soap. No luck. Vinegar, baking soda, BonAmi—maybe the tattoos were a bit lighter, but those elderberries had left their mark. For the next two days we occupied ourselves with practically scrubbing our skin off.

Our efforts paid off. On the first day of school, although we still wafted "Essence of Fels Naptha", the tattoos were too light for anybody to notice.

Elderberries are nothing but trouble.

TRIVIA

Questions:

1. Name three other foods that country people canned

2. What was one of the best-known names for canning supplies?

3. How did you know if a jar was really sealed?

Answers:

1. Pickles, meat, vegetables . . .

2. Ball, Mason, Kerr

3. The raised button on the lid went down

THE REFINED LOOK
(A city story by Jon)

I don't know when knickers went out of style, but I can tell you that in the fall of nineteen forty-four when I was nine, practically every guy in my class was wearing khakis. The war was on, and we were dressing like our servicemen. The only boy condemned to wearing funny-looking knee-length pants and argyle socks was my best friend, Bubby Burley.

I thought knickers were a fashion has-been, but Bubby never complained about them to his friends. If he pushed his imagination to the limit, he could pretend he was a big-time football player, and what was wrong with that? On the other hand, word got around that Bub complained regularly to his mother that his knickers were itchy and funny looking.

Well, that was Bubby's problem, not mine--until one fateful evening in early September, just before school started. My mother wanted to look at Fiesta Ware dishes at Philadelphia Sales, our discount department store. Maybe there was another Philadelphia Sales store in Philadelphia, but the "Philly Sales" in Binghamton, New York was just a few miles from our house.

"Come with us, Jon," my mother said. "I bet your dad will get you some popcorn."

Who could resist?

I piled into the back seat of our gray '36 Plymouth. My dad cranked the window down, and the smoke from his Pall-Mall cigarette wafted pleasantly around me. The air was warm and balmy, and the noise and fumes of the rush hour had passed. We rolled right along until we arrived at the back parking lot of the gray, tattered building that housed Philly Sales.

The back entrance to the store smelled like the lobby of a movie theater, and it probably sold as much popcorn. While my mother was shopping, I planned to share a bagful with my dad.

"Come on, Jon," my mother said. "Let's look around."

"I don't care about dishes," I said, situating myself next to the popcorn machine.

"Oh, they sell other things, too," she said. "Come on with me."

We went straight to the boys' department.

"I thought I'd look at some new trousers for you while we're here," she said. You've grown tall this summer. Now, stay with me for a few minutes while I look."

I headed straight for the khakis. She headed straight for a sales rack.

"Jon! Come here! I've found the perfect thing!" she said, beaming like she had discovered gold hiding among the clothes.

She had found knickers--not just one pair, but two. Not just two pairs of knickers, but a matching jacket.

"Look. Beautiful navy wool serge!" she said, fingering the jacket.

"The guys aren't wearing knickers," I said. "They're wearing khakis."

"I noticed your friend Bubby wearing knickers," my mother said. "They look so much more refined than those khakis."

"Jack wears them every day."

"I know," she said. "But your brother happens to be in the Marines. He doesn't have a choice."

"If he did have a choice, he'd stick with his khakis," I argued.

My mother wasn't listening. She handed the knickers and jacket to me.

"Now, go in the dressing room and try them on," she said. "I'll get some socks to go with them."

Okay. I'd try them on--me, with my broomstick legs. She'd see how awful they looked. Bubby had broomstick legs, too. The wide striped elastic cuffs that were supposed to fit snugly below his knees hung loose and shapeless and the argyle socks that he wore with them were always bunched around his ankles. I'd look just like Bubby.

I pulled the skimpy yellow curtain across the dressing room opening, slipped off my shorts, and put on my new clothes, bunching my socks so my mother would get the full effect. If she was looking for a refined look, she wasn't going to find it with me wearing knickers.

My mother thought I looked adorable.

She paid for the suit and socks, and then she handed the bag of new clothes to me.

"Now, go find your father," she said. "Tell him I'm going to get the Fiesta Ware now."

My father was a quiet guy. When I showed him my new outfit, he didn't say a word. He raised his eyebrows, and then he bought me a bag of popcorn.

My mother returned from the house wares section with her second fabulous find of the night--a round green Fiesta Ware pitcher, perfect, she told my father, for iced tea.

We were ready to go home.

Gloomily I followed my parents to the car, my buttery treat in one hand, and the bag of has-been fashion in the other.

My father turned on the car radio so I could listen to Henry Aldrich, but for once I didn't even laugh. I couldn't get my mind off those knickers. Nothing could be worse.

I was wrong. In November, my mother bought me arctics--those black rubber boots with buckles. Every school morning, I hurried up the street, clomping along in my boots, until I came to Bub's house. Then, I left them on his porch for the day.

Lucky for me, I was just starting a growth spurt. By the time Christmas came, I had outgrown my "refined" knickers, and my mother bought khakis for me like the rest of the guys. The boots still spent their days on Bub's porch.

Poor Bub still wore his knickers. His dad was a warrant officer during the war, and in my opinion, that should have given him every right to wear khakis.

Maybe I lacked refinement, but I made up for it with common sense. I knew better than to share my opinion with Bub's mother.

TRIVIA

Questions:

1. What did "spotters" do during the war?

2. Name two reasons that a young man could be "deferred" and not serve in the military during the war.

3. Name a Christmas song was introduced during the war.

Answers:
1. Watched for enemy airplanes
2. Physical disability, employment vital to the war effort, religious beliefs
3. White Christmas, I'll Be Home For Christmas ...

WELCOMING THE LIGHT

Every year on September 21, my mother hung her battered almanac by its string on the latch of the Hoosier cabinet. On that day, our family's warrior of darkness, like a sentry spying on the enemy, began to keep a stern eye on Mother Nature as she stole away the daylight, minute by minute.

In the remaining days of September, sixteen minutes of daylight were stolen. Mother could live with that; we could eat dinner and get the dishes washed before 6:27 with no need to light the lamp. In October, we lost an hour and twenty-seven minutes.

The time had come to outwit the solar system. There was no need to light the lamp over the kitchen table yet, but we needed to see to wash the dishes.

Mother knew a trick to solve that problem. We adjusted dinnertime, sitting down at the table at 4:45 and hustling through our meal so we could still see to clean up the kitchen.

In November, Mother Nature won the battle. By 4:10, darkness crept into every corner of our little house. The shiny nickel trim on the cook stove relinquished its luster, and the black cat, sleeping underneath, seemed to wrap herself in it, like a cozy blanket. Mother grimly cleaned the lamp chimneys with newspapers every day, determined to squeeze every ounce of candlepower from the kerosene lamps. She lit the reflector lamp above the clock shelf, but, even at its shiny best, it was no match for the darkness.

The time had come for Mother to admit defeat.

At dinnertime, she lowered the iron horse lamp from its place near the ceiling and placed a lamp inside its flowery pale pink shade. How beautiful that hanging lamp was! How lovely my family looked, bathed in the dim glow that it shed around the table!

The mismatched plates and cups and saucers, the hodgepodge silverware, always properly arranged with the fork on the left, the knife and spoon on the right, and the jelly glasses of milk for us children, all resting on the flowered oilcloth--all beautiful--but I couldn't tell my mother. She was locked in a battle with the solar system, and in no mood to appreciate the loveliness of our dinner table.

Even for us children, the dark days of winter weren't always sweetness and light.

When it was time to clean up the dishes, we couldn't see what we were doing. If someone placed a lamp close to the dishpan and a drop of water splashed on the chimney, it cracked, and that was the end of it. It couldn't be used again. When we finished the dishes, we couldn't see to put them away in the dark pantry

Another problem was sock matching. On those dark mornings, we'd reach for a pair of socks, but by the light of the lamp, we couldn't tell if we had selected two pinks, two yellows, or one pink and one yellow. How embarrassed we felt, walking into school looking like clowns.

We couldn't help ourselves--we complained to Mother. She had no sympathy. She had troubles of her own.

She helped with the milking by the dim light of a lantern. She couldn't see to sew in the evening, or catch up on the ironing, or straighten a kitchen drawer. The solar system was winning the battle.

In December, Mother was given a reprieve. December 21, the day of the winter solstice arrived, and our fighter began her victory lap.

"Seven more minutes of daylight this month," she'd say, "And by the end of January, we'll have daylight at 5:00."

She couldn't wait that long. Around the middle of January, she pushed the iron horse lamp back up near the ceiling, and at 4:45 our family gathered around the table for dinner.

TRIVIA

Questions:

1. How is a lamp wick trimmed?

2. A carelessly trimmed wick causes what problems?

3. A lamp chimney can be removed when it's still hot by grasping it in what way?

Answers:

1. Straight across with scissors

2. Poor light and a smoky chimney

3. At the base of the chimney

SHOPPING AT JONES'S

My big sister got a new boyfriend. I don't know if he really took a shine to the twins and me, or if he was just trying to impress my sweet teenaged sibling. It didn't matter; he reached in his pocket and doled out three nickels, one for each of us.

I was rich! I spent that warm summer Sunday clutching my money and considering what I might buy at Jones's gas station the next day.

I was only six, and I had never been to Jones's. The other sisters made the two-mile round trip when they got a little money, but until that day, my mother had thought I was too small to go. Now, here I was, suddenly wealthy, and with pressing business to tend to.

Jones's gas station existed long before President Eisenhower decided to create the interstates. Situated close to the shoulder on New York State Route 11, it consisted of two gas pumps and a tiny store that was part of Mrs. Jones's kitchen.

Here are a few things I didn't know when I set off down our shady dirt road with the twins the next day:

Is ginger ale an alcoholic beverage? Did it cost a nickel? If I bought it, how would it taste? What did coke taste like?

Did Mrs. Jones have penny candy? Never mind the licorice sticks. What about b-b bats, all day suckers, cinnamon buttons, tiny wax bottles filled with sugary liquid, candy cigarettes, packs of caramels, and sticks of gum, five to a package. I knew she sold small cups of ice cream, complete with flat wooden spoons. My imagination stretched that nickel to include them all.

Sweaty and dusty, my sisters and I stepped into Mrs. Jones's store.

A glass-fronted cabinet mounted high on a wall displayed the merchandise.

Alas, the selection was limited to candy bars, gum, cigarettes, chewing tobacco, bread, and motor oil.

Two little boys wearing diapers and bibs toddled out to stare at us. Three older girls that we saw in school almost every day stood near the kitchen table and studied us without a word. I squeaked out a shy "Hi" and one of them nodded. We all seemed out of place.

I walked into an alcove and examined the bottles of soda pop. I looked at the ice cream. I might have selected that, but I didn't know how much it cost and I was afraid to ask. I couldn't take a chance on the soda pop because I didn't know the price, and besides, what if I didn't like it? A whole nickel wasted, if that was what it cost.

A car drove up to the gas pumps, and Mrs. Jones walked out to insert the nozzle into the gas tank and crank the handle to pump the gas.

I looked at the candy bars: Hershey, Babe Ruth, and Bit-O-Honey. I was fairly sure one would cost a nickel, but I knew myself--I'd gobble it down in five bites.

With my newly acquired reading skills I studied the cigarettes and tobacco: Camel, Lucky Strike, and Chesterfield. Red Man, Beechnut, and Uncle Sam.

The twins were considering the gum. Juicy Fruit, Spearmint, Black Jack, or Chiclets. Bev chose Juicy Fruit, Bea selected Spearmint, and I bought the Chiclets. To my way of thinking, they were a better buy. There were ten in a package, and they'd last longer, if I could control my temptations. Besides, someone had shared a few with me before, and I remembered the feel of their smooth, hard outer shells when I shook them in my hand.

We parted with our nickels and thanked Mrs. Jones.

As we started up our dirt road, the twins opened their gum and stuffed all five pieces in their mouths.

"You chew like old cows," I said.

"That's how you're supposed to chew gum," Bea said. "Now, eat all of yours."

I didn't. I helped myself to one piece and put the rest in my pocket. My gum would last.

"Come on, let's run," Bev said.

We all took off running. Somehow my precious Chiclets flew out of my pocket and got lost in the weeds along the road. We searched and searched, but we never found them.

The twins chewed their gum until it lost its flavor, and then they rolled it in the sugar bowl when mother wasn't looking and chewed it some more. As for me, by the time my tiny Chiclet lost its flavor there wasn't enough left to roll in the sugar bowl.

TRIVIA

Questions:

1. What was the approximate cost of gasoline in the early 1940's?

2. Today we have a selection of regular, high test, premium.... what were the options then?

3. When was unleaded gas introduced?

Answers:
1. About fifteen cents gallon
2. Regular and high test
3. The 1970's

STICK-AND-BREAD-DOUGH BATONS

By nineteen forty-three, most of the farmers in our neighborhood were boosting themselves out of the depression. John Deere, McCormack, Alice Chalmers, and Oliver tractors hummed in the fields, and electric lights shone from farmhouse windows at night.

There were a few countrymen like my father, though, who still used workhorses to till the soil and harvest their crops, and who lived too far out in the country to hook up to electricity. Somehow, these men and their families simply couldn't find their way out of the depression, and they continued to scrabble and struggle and "make do" for years to come.

In their own way, the children "made do" too. Most of the time, however, this making-do involved elaborate plans and wild imaginations, and the results were well worth any deprivation that got the idea rolling in the first place.

The twins were ten and I was eight when we saw two high school girls twirling their batons in a performance in our school auditorium. The stage footlights shone like jewels, reflecting off the girls' glittery costumes and their flashing, spinning batons. A scratchy recording of "You're A Grand Old Flag" played in the background. The girls flung their batons in the air and caught them. They passed them behind their necks and backs and between their legs.

Sometimes, they twirled a baton in each hand. Their performance was glorious.

When we got off the bus and started up our dirt road that afternoon, the twins discussed our situation. We needed batons. We needed footlights. We needed music. We needed an audience.

The twins' imaginations began to perk.

As soon as we got in the house, we ditched our lunch boxes, changed our clothes and raced to the woods.

"Look for a straight stick with no bark on it, Short," Bea said. "Twirl it under your arm and around to be sure it's the right length."

I picked up a stick

"Under and around? How?"

Bea sighed.

"A person would think you didn't even see those baton twirlers today," she said.

"Never mind. I'll find a stick for you."

She found a silver-gray one that was reasonably straight, and showed me how to twirl it so I could be sure it was the right size.

Bea found one for herself, and Bev discovered a good one, too, and we raced back to the house.

Mother was putting bread in pans, forming the dough into perfect loaves.

Bev stopped in her tracks.

"Mom, if you'd give us each a ball of bread dough, we could make a beautiful performance for you," she said.

"I'd like that," Mother said, and she presented each of us with some dough.

"Get the glass doll dishes, Short," Bea told me. "We can use the yellow plates for footlights."

After we lined up the plates on the living room floor, we turned our attention to the bread dough. As usual, I followed the twins' lead: Break it in half, roll it into two balls, and press the balls onto the baton ends. Those twins had wonderful ideas!

The time had come to invite our audience. Bev called Mother into the living room, and we lined up behind our footlights. The performance began.

We twirled and spun, and the bread dough flew around the room. It landed on Mother's sewing machine and in Dad's brown chair. It landed on the pot-bellied stove and on the sofa.

The performance came to a halt. We retrieved our baton ends and tied them on with string, but the dough flew off again. Then, Bea flung her baton into the air, and when it came down it broke one of the glass doll dishes.

"Never mind," Bea said. "We'll stand behind the footlights and sing and dance."

We skipped around and shook our heads to make our hair swirl while we sang, "You're A Grand Old Flag" and Mother clapped and clapped.

The performance was over.

We collected the bread dough and made a loaf of bread for mother to bake for the dog.

"If we'd had better batons we could have really twirled," Bev said as she swept the broken doll dish into the dustpan."

"Yeah," Bea agreed. "We needed something more silver. We should have looked for better sticks."

As for me, I knew that the grand baton-twirling scheme was over. We would never search for better sticks or baton ends, and we'd never again substitute doll dish plates for footlights.

The twins had moved on.

TRIVIA

Questions:

1. What are baton twirlers called?
2. What objects besides batons are or have been twirled?
3. What are baton ends made of? (Not bread dough!)

Answers:
1. Majorettes
2. Knives, guns, swords, sticks
3. Rubber

POTATO PICKING

Every year my father planted potatoes--not just a couple of rows, but acres of them. With eleven kids in the family, our parents relied heavily on those belly-fillers, and we enjoyed them at least once a day the year round. We ate them scalloped, baked, creamed, boiled, mashed, hash-browned, and home-fried. If I was hungry enough, I ate some raw with salt and pepper.

Potatoes were cheap to grow, especially if you cut most of your seed potatoes from last year's leftovers. My father used a horse-drawn planter to put the seed potatoes in the ground, so he didn't need help with that. He didn't need help with his crop in the summer, either; mostly, the plants took care of themselves. In the fall, however, when it was time to pick the potatoes, Dad loaded us children on the lumber wagon, and off we went to the potato field, squeezed in with bushel baskets and feed sacks, bumping along a rutted log road through our woods to the ten acres of cleared land where the potatoes waited.

Kid help is perfect for potato picking. It's not a skilled job, kids have strong young backs, and they'll work for free if they're your kids. If you're blessed with gullible little daughters, well, then, you have a truly enviable crew.

I liked our October rides along the log road. The leaves had fallen by then, and the wet ruts in the old track smelled heavy and pungent with decaying vegetation. Partridge thundered up from under the beeches, and migrating geese honked in the bright blue sky. Rabbits dove for cover, and sometimes we heard a deer crashing through the underbrush.

Life was good until Dad turned the team into the potato field.

He unhitched the horses from the wagon, hitched them to the potato digger, and started down a row, exposing the new potatoes, clustered under the dead vines like nests of eggs. Armed with bushel baskets, we began to work.

The first hour of picking was easy. The sun wasn't too hot, our backs weren't stiff, the dust that was kicked up from the digger hadn't got on our nerves yet, and the novelty of the job hadn't worn off. By afternoon, however, Dad's cheap and unskilled laborers had had enough. My sisters and I were hot and dusty, our backs were stiff, and our hands were caked with dirt from the potatoes. Also, by four o'clock the sun was sinking in the sky, and the air was turning cold.

That didn't matter to Dad. Up and down the rows he went, riding along on the digger, turning up more and more potatoes. We didn't dare to stop; Dad said potatoes couldn't stay out in the sun very long or they'd get sunburned— that's the green discoloration that you still find on potatoes today.

We were slowing down--really slowing down. We couldn't seem to help it.

Dad stopped the team, took his Red Man tobacco from his hip pocket, and helped himself to a chew. He picked up two potatoes and put them in a basket.

"Did I ever tell you about Uncle Will?" he asked. "He was my dad's brother. He died before you kids were born."

He spat tobacco juice into a pile of dead potato vines.

"Well, Uncle Will was over here plowing one spring, and he lost his pocket watch."

Dad shook his head and lowered his chin so we'd appreciate the seriousness of his story.

"Well," he continued, "Uncle Will looked and looked, but he never found it. Someday, it's bound to turn up, with all the plowing and digging I do over here. It was fourteen carat gold, so it'll be worth something. Whoever finds it, well—'finder's keepers', that's what I say."

We bent over the potatoes again, picking fast, eager to keep moving on and looking for the watch. Our imaginations were galloping.

If I found it, I planned to sell it and get a bathroom put in our house, and if there were any money left over, I'd buy a typewriter. If there was still money left over--well!

My sisters worked steadily beside me, lost in their thoughts, probably making their plans for the watch, too.

Nobody found it.

At the end of the day, Dad loaded the potatoes on the wagon, and his weary helpers perched on lumpy potato sacks, and rode back along the log road to the house.

The workday still wasn't over. Dad pulled the team around to the outside cellar door, and we helped him unload the potatoes into the freshly cleaned potato bin.

Finally, we dragged into the kitchen for supper. We dined on slab bacon, homemade bread, canned corn, and---potatoes!

TRIVIA

Questions:

1. What are the "seeds" of a potato?
2. How did farmers know when the potatoes were ready to dig?
3. What was the rule for cutting seed potatoes?

Answers:

1. The eyes

2. The vines died

3. An eye in every piece

THE SUNSHINE BOX

We were blotchy little prisoners, lying in the dark in Mother's bedroom with the door closed.

"Don't raise the shades," Mother cautioned. "You'll ruin your eyes."

So, there we were--three grumpy little girls in bed with the measles, with nothing to do except argue and mutter and scratch our itchy welts. We didn't feel very sick.

"Quit hogging the quilts!" Bea said.

"How can I be hogging the quilts?" I said. "All I have is one little corner."

"If you two would stop wiggling and kicking, the bed wouldn't be such a mess and you'd both have plenty of quilts," said Bev. "Now, get out of the bed, and I'll make it again."

"I don't want you to make it," I said. "You're too fussy, and after you make it, all you do is squawk at me for moving a little bit."

"Oh, we'll get out," Bea said. "Bev can make the bed twenty times a day, and who cares?"

We climbed out, and Bev smoothed the sheets, straightened the quilts, and shook the pillows before she told us we could get back in.

"And be careful," Bev said. "Don't mess it up when you get in. And lie perfectly straight, and I'll spread the quilts over you."

Bea hopped into the bed, arms and legs flailing, shaking her head from side to side on the perfect pillows.

"Get out!" Bev hollered. "Both of you!"

Mother came to the bedroom door.

"Girls! Girls!" she said. "All of you get in that bed, lie down and rest. All you have is the three-day measles. They'll be gone in no time. If it weren't for protecting your eyes, I'd send you all outside, and I don't care if it is March and still cold."

Then she said, "Goodness!" and went back to the kitchen.

Mother had had enough.

We quietly climbed back in bed.

"Car's coming," Bea whispered. "Listen."

Since our house was the only one on our dirt road, we were pretty sure we were going to have company.

A car door slammed.

We heard feet in the woodshed.

"David!"

"It's Dave!" Bev said. "Wonder what he's doing here."

"Oh, David, what a wonderful surprise!" Mother said. "What brings you here today, son?"

"I got your postcard," our brother said. "I brought something for my sick sisters."

Dave opened the bedroom door, strode to the window, and raised the shade.

"You kids look terrible," he said. "No wonder Mother is keeping it dark in here. Nobody can stand to look at you."

"David," Mother said, "Don't raise the shade. We have to be careful of their eyes."

"I'll be right back," Dave said. "Don't lower the shade for a minute."

Bev, Bea and I were wiggling and squirming and kicking off the quilts.

Dave came back into the bedroom carrying a box covered in yellow crepe paper.

We knew what it was--a sunshine box!

Sometimes, if a kid at school got really sick with appendicitis or pneumonia or some other terrible disease, a teacher, or sometimes the bus driver, would cover a cardboard grocery box with crepe paper and kids would fill it with candy bars, small toys, hand lotion, fresh fruit, and small books, and the box would be delivered to our ailing classmate.

We were never sick, so we never got one.

Here we were, hardly sick at all, and our brother had brought one for us.

"Go ahead, you nosey kids, look inside," Dave said.

We found paper dolls, Lifesavers, oranges, small black and white magnetic Scottie dogs, combs for each of us, coloring books and new crayons, and games covered in clear plastic with b-b's inside, and pictures with holes to accommodate the b-b's. Move the b-b's into the eye holes, the nose hole, the mouth, make the buttons on the man's shirt--not an easy task, because if you wiggled too much the b-b's rolled out of the places you had managed to get them into.

"Okay," Dave said, lowering the shade. "You've seen enough. Now, lie down and be quiet."

"Wait! Wait," I hollered. "I didn't see everything."

"You saw enough," Dave said. "Here, I'll give you each an orange, and you'll have to wait for the rest until you get well."

Dave closed the bedroom door.

"Let's see how many times we can throw our oranges in the air and catch them," Bev said.

Mine was the first to roll under the bed.

Bea's came down and landed on Bev's forehead, so Bev got mad. Bea said it wasn't her fault because she couldn't see.

Then Bev's orange joined mine somewhere under the bed, and Bea said she couldn't play without us.

We went back to our grumpy, measly selves, until in a few days, our prison door swung open, and we were free to enjoy the sunshine box.

TRIVIA

Questions:

1. How many times do most people get the three-day measles?

2. What is the medical name for three-day measles?

3. What is yet another name for three-day measles?

Answers:

1. Usually just once

2. Rubella

3. German measles

THE ENGAGEMENT

"You wanna get engaged?"

That's the question all young girls dream of hearing. Forget commitment--I didn't even know the word. Just give me the ring!

I was eight years old the first time a certain man slipped a ring on my finger. He was an ancient fellow, somewhere in his forties, with a wife and children, and he was betrothed to every little girl in the neighborhood whose family had horses. Never mind that the rings were made from horseshoe nails, and the man smelled of sweat and horseflesh and smoke from his forge. Pay no attention to the fact that he came to our house just twice a year. What could one expect from a farrier?

My sisters, the twins, were only ten, and they were anxious to get engaged, too. We knew, though, that our engagements were based, not on love, but on patience, and every time the farrier came up our road, we settled in for a long wait.

He arrived in the evening, trailing clouds of dust as he rattled up our dirt road. As soon as he parked his truck under the big maple in the side yard, we girls drifted outside to watch him unload his forge and fire it up. Then he brought out his nippers, clippers, and rasps, pails of horseshoes and nails, his tongs and hammer, and the anvil, and arranged them on the tailgate. Occasionally, he held up a rasp and asked if we girls wanted a manicure, but usually he paid no attention to us at all.

When Dad brought out the team, our suitor tied his heavy, greasy apron around his ample waist, and the work began. "Foot!" he'd say. "Foot!" Somehow, the horses understood their role in the process, and they obligingly lifted whatever foot he wanted. Then, while the new shoes heated to red hot on the forge, he cradled each hoof against his apron, and clipped, snipped and filed. With his tongs, he placed a hot horseshoe against a hoof, and then formed it on his anvil to fit perfectly. Then he nailed it on. Eight shoes. Three little girls, waiting.

When the shoeing was finished, our farrier dumped the coals from his forge onto the ground and loaded his equipment into his truck. Last of all—oh, no!--he loaded his anvil, hammer and horseshoe nails, the tools of his jewelry making.

We waited while Dad and the farrier leaned against the truck and discussed gravels, spavins, bruises, the heaves, and every possible ailment of horses. Finally, Dad led the team back to the barn.

The sun was setting when the farrier finally turned to us and popped the question:

"You girls wanna get engaged?"

Oh, yes, we did! We extended our hands, and he peered at our ring fingers in the fading light. After a careful look, he reached into his truck and retrieved three nails and his hammer. Then, sliding the anvil onto the tailgate, he formed a ring for each of us. He tried them on our fingers, adjusted the size, and slid them on again. When at last they were perfect, he blew on them and polished them on a clean patch of his shirttail before placing them on our fingers for the final time.

"There we go," he said. "We're engaged."

How elegant we felt! We extended our hands as far from our faces as possible. A person who didn't know would probably mistake those nail heads for real diamonds.

A few weeks later, the arguments began: "That's my ring, no, it's mine, it's mine!" Then, mother took our rings away. We consoled ourselves with the knowledge that in six months the farrier would return and get around to popping the question again.

TRIVIA

Questions:

1. Why did countrymen have their horses shod in the fall?

2. Name two methods of attaching horseshoes

3. Why do people nail horseshoes over barn doors?

Answers:

1. The farrier added cleats to the horseshoes to prevent slipping on ice and snow

2. Nails and glue

3. For good luck

THE CURE
(A city story by Jon)

I jumped out of bed and practically flew into my parents' room.

"Eeeh! Eeeh!" I gasped, clutching my throat and struggling to inhale.

My parents jumped out of bed and practically flew into my grandmother's room, with me behind them, gasping for air.

When Gram heard me she got out of bed and hustled downstairs to the kitchen. Cupboard doors banged and dishes rattled. Gram was cooking up a concoction, and an ominous odor was already creeping up the stairs.

"She's making you a mustard plaster," Dad said. "You'll feel better in no time."

When Gram came back up the stairs, she was carefully carrying a flannel cloth. The dry, bitter odor of mustard escaped from its folds.

"Go back to bed, Jon," she said. "I'll take care of you."

I did as I was told. My mother unbuttoned my pajama top and Gram applied the plaster to my chest.

I could breathe! Oh, could I breathe! My nostrils, my sinuses, my throat were invaded with hot mustard fumes. If I'd been old enough to have chest hairs, that vile plaster would have burned them off.

Gram waited for a few minutes, lifted the plaster, and examined my chest.

"Not quite yet," she said. She waited a few more minutes and examined my chest again.

"There, now," she said, removing the cloth.

"Better?" she asked cheerfully.

"Yeah." She had practically killed me, but I had to admit she sure had cured me.

"What's in that cloth, anyway?" I asked.

Four tablespoons of dry mustard, two of flour, and enough water to make a nice paste," Gram said. "Would you like me to unfold it and let you smell it?"

"Nah. That's okay," I said.

"Well, then, go to sleep," she said.

Dad spread my quilt over me, my mother kissed me goodnight, and Gram hurried off with her poultice.

The good news, I thought, was I wouldn't be going to school in the morning.

Thanks to that mustard plaster, though, my mother roused me at seven o'clock, the way she always did.

"Time to get ready for school. You're fine now," she said.

When I turned sixteen, I got a job, clerking at the local drug store.

One day, I noticed a mustard plaster tucked away in a drawer.

"My grandmother made one of those and put it on my chest one night when I couldn't breathe," I said.

The pharmacist was horrified. "Oh!" he said, "Did it burn you?"

"No."

"No blisters?"

"No.

"Well, you're lucky," he said. "Those things are nasty business. If they touch your bare skin, they'll burn you and even blister you. That one in the drawer has been around since the beginning of time. People don't use them anymore."

I wanted to ask what people did when their kid woke up in the night unable to breathe, but I thought better of it. If I ever grew up and had a kid who couldn't get a breath, I knew what I'd do. I was living proof that mustard plasters worked.

TRIVIA

Questions:

1. Name two items that could be purchased in a 1940's and 50's drug store to take care of our ailments.

2. Name two drug store items that were used then and are still used

3. Name any kind of poultice

Answers:

1. Smith Bros cough drops, Mercurochrome, iodine, Unguentine

2. ExLax, Vicks. Oil of cloves, Oil of peppermint, band aids

3. Bread and milk poultice, onion poultice, catnip poultice . . .

THE UMBRELLA

When I was nine my family had the good fortune to acquire an umbrella. It came in a box from our city cousin, along with her children's outgrown clothes.

The pink and purple plaid umbrella was gorgeous. I couldn't wait to carry it down our dirt road, twirl it prettily until the school bus came to a stop, and then fold it demurely like the fine lady I secretly was.

There were some flaws in my plans.

First, the umbrella wasn't mine. Like most treasures at our house, the beautiful umbrella was something I'd have to share with my sisters, the twins, Bev and Bea. Second, my lovely springtime accessory arrived at the beginning of winter.

To complicate my life a little more, my cousin, Jean, moved in with us that year. Now, there'd be four schoolgirls who'd be expected to share the umbrella.

The only problem that resolved itself was the winter season. By late March the weather turned balmy, and one morning I awoke to the sound of a spring rain.

I hurried through breakfast and rushed to claim the umbrella. Almost as soon as I brought it from Mother's bedroom, the twins and Jean were at my elbows.

"I'll carry that," Jean said. "I had one once, and I know how to use it. Besides, I'm the tallest."

"Okay," Bev said, "But don't you try to hog it."

We stepped out into the rain, and Jean opened the umbrella.

I got behind her, the twins arranged themselves on either side of her, and we started slowly down the muddy road.

"Well, Jean," Bea said, "It would be nice if you could share a tiny bit of the umbrella with me. All I'm getting are the drips from it."

"I'd do better if your little sister"--Jean glared over her shoulder at me—"would quit walking on the backs of my shoes. She's practically pulling them off."

"I can't help it," I said. "It's the only way I can stay out of the rain."

"Jean," Bev said. "I think you should know I slept on metal curlers last night, just so my hair would look good today. Now, the right side is soaking wet and straight as a board. I guess you know whose fault that is."

Jean was quiet for a moment. Then she said, "Okay, somebody else can carry this darn umbrella."

"Well, I can't," I said. "Everybody knows I'm too short."

The twins were silent. Finally, Bev said, "Jean, we don't change horses in mid-stream around here. You wanted to carry it, and we let you. Now, keep going."

We struggled down the road to the bus stop, glowering and muttering as we walked.

When Jean saw the bus coming, she folded the umbrella and shoved it into my hands.

"Here," she said. "You can carry the darn thing on the bus."

Well, she could call the umbrella anything she wanted. All my dreams and fantasies had been destroyed.

Glumly I carried the darn thing onto the bus.

TRIVIA

Questions:

1. Give another name for an umbrella

2. In what country were the first folding umbrellas used?

3. What is the main difference between a parasol and an umbrella?

Answers:

1. A bumbershoot

2. China

3. An umbrella is waterproof and designed to protect from the rain. A parasol is not waterproof and is designed to protect from the sun

APPLES

Some modern families think an apple orchard is a place to visit in October, when the Macintoshes. Granny Smiths and Cortlands are as crisp and cold as the day itself, and the air is rich with the scent of apples, spiced with a blend of fall leaves and wood smoke. Even if there's no wood fire for miles around, grownups think they can smell one.

Families fill their car trunks with bags of red, yellow, and green apples, and on their way home, maybe they'll stop to buy some pumpkins and Indian corn. For these folks, that's all they need to know about apple orchards and apples.

My family's orchard was a treasure that spanned all four seasons. When the apple trees decorated the meadow with blossoms my sisters and I, so weary of winter cold and snow and April rain and mud, knew we could finally, officially, welcome springtime. In August the wormy yellow transparents ripened. I like to think we avoided every wiggly occupant of those apples and ate only the good parts, but we were hungry children lured to a tree full of the first apples of the season, and probably some of the worms got caught up in the excitement.

In the fall the "keepers" ripened--the Northern Spies, Sheeps Noses, Maiden Blush, Pound Sweets, Red Astrakhans, and Russets. These we stored in bushel baskets in the cellar.

Other apples like the Snow Apples were smaller and not good for storing, and we turned them into apple butter, apple jelly, applesauce, apple juice, and apple pie filling.

When my family had used every precious fruit the orchard had given us, we marked the end of the long season of canning and preserving, and braced ourselves for winter.

Throughout my childhood, my sisters and I often ran down to the cellar during the winter and helped ourselves to the apples. They were nothing special, they were just quick snacks to fill our bellies--until I got bogged down in sixth grade math. Then I discovered the calming properties tucked into the crunch and juice of a sheep's nose apple sprinkled with salt. It was more than calming; it was vital to my well being, to say nothing of my math grade.

Night after miserable night I sat with my math book open in front of me, paper and pencil at the ready—and—there I sat, tears welling in my eyes as I tackled the first problem: Mr. Jones has made a garden ten feet long and fifteen feet wide. (My math book showed a picture of jolly Mr. Jones in his bib overalls, leaning on his hoe.) How many square feet are in Mr. Jones's garden?

I didn't know! The teacher didn't tell me how to do this! At least I didn't think she did.

I tried the second problem. Mrs. Smith is buying a nine-by-twelve foot rug. (There's a picture of smiley Mrs. Smith holding her handbag.) It costs $1.25 a square yard. What is the price of the rug?

Well, how was I supposed to know?

I sat with trembling chin, studying the bright flowers on the kitchen table oilcloth. I, a proud honor student, was suddenly a class dunce. In the circle of light from the kerosene lamp, I watched Bev, Bea, and Shirley quietly working at the kitchen table, completing their homework.

Like all the other nights, I was stuck waiting for Dad to come in from the barn to help me.

Finally I heard him stomping the snow off his boots in the woodshed, humming 'Clementine'.

I wanted to run to the door and hug him, but we weren't a hugging family.

He came into the kitchen, set down his lantern, and hung up his hat and coat. Then he looked at me.

"What's the trouble, Short? Math again?" As if he didn't know.

I nodded.

"Why don't you take the lantern and go get us each an apple?" he said. "I'll take a Spy,"

As if he didn't choose the same kind every night.

"You get whatever you want for yourself," he added.

As if I didn't always choose a Sheep's Nose.

I was feeling better. I ran down to the dark, cold cellar and got our apples.

Dad brought the saltshaker and a plate, and we sat down at the table with the math book between us.

Calmly he took his jackknife from his pocket, the same one he used to cut plugs off his tobacco, to clean his finger-nails, to open bags of cow feed, and cut tarpaper to patch the roof. He wiped the knife on his overalls and began to cut our apples.

We sprinkled salt on some slices, took a few bites, and tackled the first problem.

"Think small, Short," Dad would say. "Give Mr. Jones a garden the size of a postage stamp. Maybe he can plant a seed or two."

Oh! I could suddenly see my teacher at the blackboard. Hmmm. I can do it!

We sprinkled more salt on our slices. Somewhere between the salt and the apple I detected the faint peppery taste of Dad's Uncle Sam plug tobacco. Right or wrong, that's how it was.

We read the second problem.

"Be careful here, Short," Dad said. "The rug is nine by twelve feet, but the price is a dollar and a quarter a yard. Now, what do you need to do?"

Oh! Now I've got it!

I wasn't a dunce after all—I was still an honor student—until I opened that math book the next night.

Then I'd turn to Dad and his jackknife and the saltshaker, and Northern Spies and Sheep's Noses, and I'd make it through another night with my honor student status still intact.

TRIVIA

Questions:

1. Name at least three desserts that feature apples

2. What is the natural ingredient in apples that makes apple jelly "jell"?

3. Name two foods or beverages that are made from apple juice

Answers:

1. Apple pie, apple crisp, baked apples, candy apples . . .

2. Pectin

3. Sweet cider, hard cider, applejack, vinegar

WHEN SNOW WHITE CAME TO TOWN

I was in the third grade when Snow White came to our small town theater.

It was the big topic of conversation in the cafeteria and on the playground. Practically everybody was going the following Friday evening.

My family didn't have a car at the time, and even if we did, I doubt our dad could have scraped together enough money to treat the whole family to the movies. Nevertheless, I joined in the Snow White excitement just like the other kids.

On Wednesday evening, my sister, Jess, and her new husband Wesley came to visit.

"We can't stay long," Jess said. "Wes has put in a long day getting corn in, and he'll put in another long day tomorrow. We just came to see if you could scare up three dimes so we can take the twins and Laura to see Snow White on Friday night."

My mother hurried to the pantry and took Dad's gold carnival glass candy dish down from the shelf. She removed its finialed cover and looked inside. "Let's see, now," she said, "It's the twenty third of October, so that means the milk check will be here in a couple of days."

Jess, the twins, and I hovered around Mother and waited.

"I think we can do it!" she announced.

She took three dimes from the candy dish and handed them to Jess.

"Okay, you kids," Jess said. "Be ready at seven o'clock Friday night."

The next day, and again on Friday, I was the most excited Snow White girl in my third grade.

On Friday night, we climbed into the rumble seat of Wes's Black Model A. Mother tucked a quilt around us, and we were off.

Bev, the worrywart, said, "I heard that if we get in an accident, the back of this rumble seat will slam shut and take our heads right off. Now, here's what we should do: If we start to get into an accident, we'll put our heads on our knees and cover the backs of our necks with our arms, okay?"

I didn't bother to answer. Snow White was waiting, and we were going to the movies for the very first time.

Bea sat with her hands clamped over her hair.

"Don't worry about our heads," she said. "Worry about whether we'll have any hair left by the time we get to the theater. That wind is awful."

We parked in the circle by the bandstand with heads and hair intact.

Jess paid for our tickets and we walked into the dim, quiet lobby of the theater. The heavy outside doors closed softly behind us, and the thick red carpet muffled our footsteps. The owner, who was also our school bus driver, nodded to Jess and shook hands with Wes. The air was heavy with the smell of popcorn.

Wes opened the inner door to the theater, and a wall of noise swelled into the lobby. So! This was where the action was! Kids were running around with bags of popcorn, spilling buttery yellow kernels on the red carpet as they raced along. Some were eating candy bars. They ran to the lobby for drinks and bathroom business. I didn't know all of them, since some were from neighboring towns that had no theaters.

"Whoa!" Wes said. "We'll go up in the balcony and get away from this noise."

The twins and I followed close behind Jess and Wes. We were in a different world, and we weren't sure how to behave.

"Five more minutes," Jess said, "The hoodlums will quiet down then and the movie will start."

Jess was a grown-up, so of course the noise bothered her. I loved it. The kids were having fun.

The lights dimmed, and the theater grew quiet.

While we watched the newsreels Wes passed along a bar of Bakers Chocolate,

We each broke off a piece and passed it back, and then we settled in to watch Snow White. Being a shy child, I especially enjoyed Bashful. He blushed like I did, but nobody ooh'd and ahhh'd for me the way they did for Bashful.

I sat in that tiny theater, my senses on high alert, absorbing the sights, sounds and smells of my first movie experience. The feel of the seats, the whir of the projector (Wes explained about that) the flickering screen, vivid with color and action, the sense of being surrounded by strangers--oh, I loved it all.

When the movie was over, we climbed back into the rumble seat, carefully stepping on the round rubber "stepping stone" and then onto the seat, and Jess tucked us in under the quilt. After such a big evening, I was tired and ready for bed, but I had a final thought before I dozed off. For the first time in my young life, I felt deep gratitude for my family--my mother who found the money in Dad's candy dish and Jess and Wes who took us to town--for all of them for arranging my grand evening at the theater.

TRIVIA

Questions:

1. Name the seven dwarfs

2. Mirror mirror on the wall . . . finish the phrase

3. Walt Disney movies cycled through theaters on a regular basis. How many years were in a cycle?

Answers:

1. Grumpy, Sneezy, Bashful, Doc, Happy, Sleepy, Dopey

2. Who's the fairest one of all

3. Seven

THE HOBO JUNGLE
(A city story by Jon)

During the early nineteen forties, we still had a place called the "hobo jungle" in our city. It was located near the river, not far from the freight yards, and also not very far from our house.

Apparently, my parents weren't very concerned about those homeless men, because they never warned me to stay away from them. I think my friends and I didn't go there because we had more interesting things to do than to walk down and pay strange, ragged men a visit. There came a night, though, when my friend, Wesley, and I visited the hobo jungle and scared ourselves half to death.

The big weekend outing for most of us kids was a trip to the Regus Theater on Saturday afternoon. Everybody called the theater "Rats Eat Garbage Under Seats", but it was within walking distance of my neighborhood, and the price of admission was just nine cents. If a kid was lucky enough to get a quarter, he could buy a ticket and then go next door to the Regus candy store and buy a five-cent bag of popcorn and six cents' worth of candy, and still have a nickel left for ice cream after the movies. Now, that was a perfect Saturday afternoon!

In the nineteen forties, the war was roaring along, and blackouts were frequent and strictly enforced. During blackouts, the city of Binghamton was as dark and quiet as a tomb.

On a sunny Saturday, Wesley and I, who were about nine, walked down to the Regus for the matinee. We bought our tickets, got our candy and popcorn, and settled down to watch Roy Rogers and Trigger straighten out the bad guys, and then fire up our imaginations with the "Lone Ranger". When the show ended, I looked over at Wesley, and there he was, sagged down in his seat, sound asleep.

I tried to wake him up, but Wesley was dead to the world.

The theater was almost empty. I had no idea of the time, but I knew I should be on my way home. I tried again to rouse Wesley, but he wouldn't rouse.

I couldn't leave him.

I sat there like a faithful dog and waited until, finally, Wesley woke up.

I hurried him out of the dark theater and onto the sidewalk. Night had fallen, and the entire city was as dark as the inside of a walnut. We were having a blackout.

The only light I could see was a flashlight carried by an air raid warden. He was busily looking for any telltale crack of light that was escaping from behind shades or draperies. If he spotted a light, he rapped on the door. "Lights out!" he'd say.

The warden wasn't interested in a couple of scared kids.

My heart started to pound. I needed to get home!

"Come on, Wesley," I said.. "We're going to take the shortcut through the hobo jungle."

Wesley started to cry.

"I'm scared," he blubbered. "I'm scared."

"Well, don't be," I said. "They're just a bunch of men. We'll be through there in no time if we run."

When we got to the jungle, we took off running. Smoke from fires and cigarettes hid the faces of the men, and I was sure I smelled booze. The hobos didn't make a move toward us or say a word, but we didn't slow down.

Five minutes later, Wesley went racing across the bridge to his house, and I flew in the back door of mine, sweaty and out of breath, and immensely grateful for the safety of my still-darkened house and my family.

TRIVIA

Questions:

1. What had happened to a hobo who had "Caught the Westbound"?

2. Name an entertainer of the '50's who played a hobo character

3. Name a hobo song

Answers:

1. He had died

2. Red Skelton as Freddie the Freeloader or Emmett Kelly as Weary Willie

3. Big Rock Candy Mountain, King of the Road, Hallelujah I'm a Bum. . .

OPERATOR

In today's world, phones are a fact of life. Youngsters walk along, tapping the keys, dialing and texting, checking their mail, and confirming the strength of their batteries. Modern folks can't be seen in public without a phone at their ear or ringing and vibrating in their pockets.

I'm almost embarrassed to confess that I reached the ripe old age of sixteen before I answered the black tabletop phone at my brother's house. I'm even more embarrassed to confess I was scared. With heart pounding and head in a whirl I said shakily, "Hello?"

"Is Thelma there?" a neighbor asked.

I was too shaken to even see if the little girl was in my brother's yard.

"No, she's not," I answered. Then I hung up the phone. Whew!

Within a few months, I learned to love that phone. Every night after school I called my friends or even waited for a (ahem) boy to call me. Phones weren't scary, they were magic. I didn't give a thought to what happened after I spun the numbers around on that rotary dial and my friend's phone rang at the other end.

Then, one wintry Saturday morning in 1953, I went with my brother to visit a woman in the tiny town of Chenango Forks, New York. There, right in the middle of her dining room, was the community switchboard--an unwieldy polished oak "conversation piece" about three feet wide, five feet high and three feet deep. AT&T stood at the ready, waiting to answer your call with a businesslike "Operator", then "Thank you" as you got connected.

I stood behind Beatrice Peterson, the homeowner and head operator, as she plugged in the cables, watched for the red lights that told her the call had been completed, and then, with a brisk pull and a snap, she disconnected the cables from their little holes and let them drop back into their holders.

Then a buzz and a white light. Another call. "Operator. Thank you." Beatrice plugged in a cable and pushed a lever to "ring" the phone of the person receiving the call. Lights kept flashing. She plugged in, answered, plugged in again and answered.

"Operator. Thank you."

"Oh, Beatrice, what a perfect job!" I said. My love affair with phones was in full bloom. What could be more wonderful than talking on one all day?

Keeping her eyes on the switchboard, she answered me.

"It's not what I thought it would be when I saw the ad in the paper," she said. "I thought I'd work in a building on Main Street. Imagine my surprise when the men came, drilled holes in my floor to accommodate the cables, and installed this in my dining room!"

"Operator. Thank you."

"They sure painted a nice picture," she continued. "I could stay home and watch my kids and cook meals and do laundry. The switchboard wouldn't be a problem."

"Don't worry about the nights," the men told me. "People will only call if there's an emergency."

"Huh," Beatrice said, snapping a couple of cables out of their holes and letting them drop back into their holders.

"I guess the phone company didn't know about the five beer gardens in this town."

"Around midnight this thing lights up like a Christmas tree. The drunks are calling their wives or the wives are calling the bars. Some of those men are so mean I make my husband take the calls. They're surprised to hear a male voice, let me tell you."

She answers another call. Then she continues.

"Between one o'clock when the bars close and four o'clock when the farmers get up to start their chores, it's pretty quiet. Then I get calls to the veterinarian and from farmers trying to find their hired help."

"Huh," she says. "Their hired help were probably in one of the beer gardens last night."

"At around nine o'clock," she continues, "After the kids have gone to school, the wives take over. No, I don't listen in. They're all on party lines. There are only thirteen private lines, and they're for the doctor, the druggist, the vet, the school, a few stores, and, of course, the darn beer gardens."

"Oh, I get the complaints," she said. "Somebody is monopolizing the line or somebody has been listening in to a conversation that's none of their business.".

"Since I'm the operator, the complainers want me to do something, but I stay outof it. They either work things out or they don't."

At five o'clock a high school student walks in, carrying her books. Beatrice gets up from her chair, takes off her headset and hands it to the girl, who sits down and takes a call. "Operator. Thank you."

The cables click as she plugs them in and then disconnects.

"It's better, now that I'm allowed some part-time help," Beatrice says. "A four hour break in the afternoon is such a blessing."

She sprints to her Maytag wringer washer, dumps the wet laundry into a basket, and hurries to the clothesline. She's fast, of course, and in just a few minutes, the clothes are waving in the winter breeze.

She races back to the kitchen, and the pots and pans begin to clatter. Beatrice is starting dinner.

"Don't you ever slow down?" I ask.

"After a day of sitting in that chair, it feels good to get up and move around," she says. "Besides, I still have plenty of paperwork to do for AT&T. I have to count the tickets and get them ready to go to the main office (I didn't ask what the tickets were, but maybe they were the long distance calls) then there are the trouble sheets for the maintenance men, and assigning new numbers, and keeping time sheets for the part-time help."

Beatrice laughs. "If I divide my hours by my paycheck, I'm making around twenty-five cents an hour, working around the clock, seven days a week."

"We have two hundred-eighteen subscribers, and a one-position switchboard. No matter how busy it gets, only one operator can work at a time."

Somehow, the magic of the telephone didn't seem so magic to me anymore. The curtain had been pulled away.

Beatrice kept her job for two and half years. Then AT&T built a tiny brick structure on Main Street and installed an automatic dial office. The men came and dismantled the switchboard, and at the same time, they dismantled Beatrice's life as she knew it.

"That first day, there was a deadly silence in the house," she told me. She shrugged.

"Nothing is forever," she said. "It's time to move on."

In just a few months, she and her family packed up their belongings and moved to California.

I never saw her again.

TRIVIA

Questions:

1. When phones were in their infancy, phone numbers were just four digits. As they became more popular, those digits were preceded by two ----?

2. In the 1960's, phone numbers were prefaced by three digits, called ____?

3. When people used party lines, they were encouraged to limit their conversations to how many minutes?

Answers:
1. Letters
2. The area code
3. Five

COWS AND APPLES

When I was growing up, our dairy consisted of about eight cows at any given time. Unlike today's big dairies where the animals are identified by tags in their ears, our cows were given lady names such as "Caroline" and "Mary", or descriptive names like "The Red Heifer", "Little Brown Swiss," or "Tag", because she was always the last one to come to the barn.

On most days, our cows lived up to their names. After the morning milking they ambled in single file out of the barn and down the lane to the pasture, where they spent their days enjoying such delicacies as meadow grass, dandelions and thistles. When it was time for the evening milking, the ladies returned, stepped into their assigned stanchions, ate their grain and gave their milk. Then, they walked back out of the barn and down the lane to the pasture where they resumed their grazing until it was time for the morning milking.

There always came a day in the fall, however, usually after a night of strong winds, when our cows turned into a rowdy bunch of drunks. When they didn't come to the barn for the evening milking, Dad knew they had discovered the apples in the old orchard.

"Come on, kids. You'll have to come with me and drive them back to the barn," he'd say, cutting a chew off his Red Man plug tobacco to steady his nerves.

Doris, Jessie, and Shirley, the big sisters, and Bev, Bea, and I, the little sisters, followed Dad and Mother down to the orchard. We found the cows, gorging themselves like ill-mannered children, the juice and pulp from the apples dripping out of their mouths.

Our job was to surround the herd and steer them back into the more acceptable part of the pasture, up the lane, and into the barn. It was a difficult undertaking.

The cows had no idea where they were going or why. They staggered along, bumping into one another, turning around, and wandering away from the herd. Like cow dogs-in-training, we chased and panted behind and beside them.

When they finally staggered into the barn, they couldn't find their stanchions, and again, they bumped into each other, banged into the barn doors, turned around, and tried to go back outside. With the help of the whole family, we finally got them sorted out.

"We'll have to milk 'em," Dad said. "The milk won't be any good, though. We'll have to throw it away."

"Really, Claude," said my mother, "You need to fence in that old orchard next year. This is always such a terrible evening, getting those cows in the barn and then wasting all the milk."

"You kids get some baskets and go pick up the rest of the apples and throw them over the fence," Dad said, "And next year I'll fence in the orchard."

We brought bushel baskets from the cellar, and trudged down the lane to the orchard, grumbling as we went.

"Darn cows anyway," Bev said.

"Darn apples," Bea added.

"We just got back from chasing the cows, and now we have to go pick up apples," I added.

None of us blamed Dad. We knew he'd never put a fence around the orchard, and the next fall after a windy night that blew the apples to the ground, we'd deal with drunken cows again.

Thank goodness for creative little girls! The twins and I discussed the problem and arrived at a solution.

The main issue, as we saw it, was that our drunken cows couldn't find their proper places in the barn.

The next day when the herd was grazing in the pasture, we wrote their names on their stanchions in big, penciled letters. Big letters would be easier for cows to read, of course.

When our sober, ladylike cows came to the barn that night, they had no trouble at all finding their places.

Proudly, we shared our cleverness with our parents. Dad tipped back his blue and white striped cap and scratched his head. Mother put down her milk pail and applauded. They both agreed that we had done a great job.

TRIVIA

Questions:

1. Why do cows get drunk on apples?
2. Name three breeds of cows
3. How many stomachs does a cow have?

Answers

1. The apples ferment in cows' stomachs

2. Holstein, Guernsey, Brown Swiss, Jersey, Black Angus . . .

3. Only one! It is divided into four chambers

COUNTY FAIR

I thought my teenaged sisters' boyfriends came to our house to make the twins' and my life easier and more fun. I realize now that those young men were trying their best to impress my sisters.

One boyfriend kept my old doll in working order, adjusting her eyes so they'd open and close, or reattaching dismembered arms or legs. Another boyfriend answered our questions: (What keeps the sun up there? or How do flies walk on the ceiling?) I didn't care that his answers were always the same:

"Gee, I don't know the answer to that one" or "When I go home, I'll look that up."

At least he listened to me.

One boyfriend brought maple syrup and maple candy. We talked him into turning cartwheels, and when gum fell out of his pockets, he gave it to us.

Those young men became my brothers-in-law.

A fellow named George didn't make the cut, but in my opinion, he was one of the very best. George invited the twins and me to go with him to the county fair.

Mother was puzzled.

"Why would he do that?" she said. "He doesn't know a thing about nine and eleven year old girls. He lives in a houseful of grownups."

Some may think he was trying to impress my sister, Doris. I prefer to believe he found her little sisters delightful and fascinating.

George said we'd leave right after he finished chores on Tuesday. That was children's day, so the three of us would be admitted free.

That morning, Mother brushed our hair and finished us off with big ribbons. She washed our hands and faces and helped us into our best dresses. We put on clean socks, and Mother wiped off our shoes. We were ready.

When George arrived, Mother gave him the cautionary advice that all mothers give: "Keep an eye on them, George." "When you're tired of them, just bring them back."

"And you children behave yourselves. No arguing! And do everything George says."

We were already hurrying to George's car, hopping in the back seat. We were all too shy to sit up front with George.

When we arrived at the fairgrounds, George bought a ticket for himself and parked the car, and we joined the excitement of the fair. Music blared near the midway rides, and people screamed and laughed as they whirled and spun, and finally staggered off to tackle another midway offering. The heavy smell of hot grease was like a fog around us. People were everywhere,

"Take your time," George said mildly. "We've got all day."

We walked into the Education Building. The school students of the county had filled it with entries. We found our school's submissions: A papier-mache version of the Adirondack Mountains, artwork from all the classes, instructions for hooking up a doorbell, and some first grade essays on "Why I Like My Mother". Some entries had earned blue, red, or white ribbons.

We compared our school's submissions with the others, and decided ours were the best.

We visited the Grange and 4-H Building. Handmade quilts hung from the ceiling, some proudly displaying ribbons. Baked goods were arranged on paper plates. The sultry August heat had produced green mold on most of the entries. Thank goodness the ribbons had already been awarded. The 4-H members put on a real show. They had entered lovely dresses, coats and jackets, and constructed dressing tables from orange crates set on end, with a board across the top. They had also entered paper plates of potatoes, summer squash, and corn, and displayed jars of jelly, jams, and pickles.

Every entry looked so colorful, so inspiring, so beautiful!

George walked with us, discussing the merits of each submission. He was a farmer, so he really knew about those vegetables.

In the front of the building, the Grange ladies sold pieces of pie, cake, and brownies, along with glasses of milk and lemonade.

George thought pieces of pie and glasses of milk would make a fine lunch, so we sat at an outdoor table and filled our bellies, waving away the flies as we ate.

We visited the livestock building.

Chickens, geese, cows, pigs, sheep, and horses filled the barn with their animal noises and smells. Teenagers who had entered the livestock competition had spent the night, bringing pillows and blankets from home, and sleeping on hay bales.

Several were sudsing up their animals and rinsing them with a hose.

"What's a swine, George?" I asked.

"It's a pig," George said.

Oh. I added a new word to my vocabulary.

When we'd all had our fill of the animals, we wandered back outside and along the midway.

"Come on in and watch the dancing girls!" a barker shouted. "Step right up!"

Bea, who loved music and dancing, accepted the invitation.

A lady wearing tiny shorts and a little spangled top was dancing in high-heeled shoes.

Bea was fascinated.

Our little troop stopped so Bea could watch.

"There's lots more inside the tent," the barker promised. "Come on in!"

George must have got distracted, because when he looked around, Bea was gone.

"Where's Bea?" he asked. His eyes were wide as he searched the crowd.

"She went in the tent to see the rest of the dancing girls," Bev said.

"Oh! Oh!" George gasped.

He poked his head inside the tent.

"Bea! Come on! The Ferris wheel is getting ready to start, and we need to get in line!"

"Well, okay," Bea said. "But after that, can we come back here?"

"We'll see," George told her. "But pretty soon it will be time to eat and see what's going on at the grandstand."

We never saw the dancing girls again.

George bought hot dogs and lemonade for supper, and cotton candy for dessert.

We were a little early for the grandstand entertainment, but we found what George told us were the best seats, and we watched the people trickling in, hoping to see a familiar face. We didn't.

When the entertainment began, we listened to the singers and watched the dancers, and Bea was unimpressed. She was sure those other dancing ladies were better. We watched horseback riders perform tricks and clowns being silly.

My bedtime was long past, and I was wearing down.

When the entertainment was over, we went to the car, and George started home.

As I sagged against Bev, I had one parting thought before I drifted off to sleep. George had enjoyed a wonderful day with the most delightful and fascinating companions ever.

TRIVIA

Questions:

1. What event might a fairgoer watch from the Grandstand?

2. Describe (a) a demolition derby or (b) a tractor pull

3. What special contest was held in the education building?

Answers:

1. Beauty contest, harness racing, fireworks . . .

2 (a) Old cars bump into each other until the "winner's" car is the only one still running

(b) Contestants compete to determine which tractor can pull the heaviest load

3. The spelling bee

THANK YOU, PATTI PAGE!

My family became the proud owners of our first radio in 1948, just when people in big cities were acquiring their first televisions. For us, however, our Silvertone tabletop radio with its 18"x4"x6" battery neatly tucked in the back of the console was a giant step into the modern world.

Of course, we didn't buy it. Mother was caring for two foster children, a five-year-old boy and a three year old girl. Their father, our distant cousin, whom we called "DR" decided to bring us a radio so his children could enjoy the kiddie programs, like "Big John and Sparky", as well as "The Lone Ranger", Fibber McGee and Molly", and "Amos and Andy".

As soon as DR carried the radio into the living room and set it carefully on the library table, Mother began to worry.

"How long will the batt'ry last, DR?" she wondered. "If one of the children turns it up loud, will that cause the batt'ry to give out? What about the cold? This room gets real cold in the winter," she fussed.

DR, who was hooking up the battery and antenna, turned to her and laughed.

"Irene, I want you to enjoy it," he said. "Listen to the news and the weather--here, watch this." He spun the dial. "See?" "This is WKRT out of Cortland. They'll have the local news and weather."

"Oh," said my mother, "I'd better write that number down."

"You can get Syracuse, too," DR said, "And Binghamton, and Ithaca, and sometimes, late at night, you can probably pick up the Grand Ol' Opry."

"That will be good," Mother said. "Now, DR, what is the Grand Ol' Opry?"

I stood looking over her shoulder. I knew a little about radios. My older, married sisters had them, and when I visited, I listened to whatever programs they chose, including Don McNeil's Breakfast Club, the one that began with "marching around the breakfast table". My imagination supplied the table and the people marching gaily around it. It all seemed real to me.

I didn't listen to the soap operas because my sisters thought they were silly, but I knew some of their names: Guiding Light, Our Gal Sunday, and The Romance of Helen Trent.

At night, when the men came home, their program choices scared me. The worst ones were "FBI in Peace and War", "America's Most Wanted", and "Suspense".

Now, I had my own radio, and I could make my own program choices. I forgot DR's reason for bringing us such a fine gift. Who cared about kiddie programs? Who cared about the news? I couldn't wait to twirl that dial and find the latest songs. I couldn't wait to listen to the high school basketball games. I couldn't wait for DR to go away and leave that radio to me.

At four o'clock that first day, my mother hurried to the kitchen to start dinner, admonishing me to be careful of the batt'ry. DR followed my mother.

I twirled the dial.

"Here's a request going out to Liz in Dryden from someone who knows. "Cry" by Johnny Raye."

The sad, sad strains of "Cry" filled the living room.

Wow! I didn't know the kids in Dryden, but the very idea of "someone who knows" sounded so romantic!

The next request was "The Three Bells" by The Browns for Jim Brown in McGraw. Not very romantic, but clever. Imagine that! There was really a Jim Brown in McGraw, and the song was about a Jimmy Brown.

"Riders in the Sky" by Vaughn Monroe was next. Some girl requested it for herself, just because she liked it. How annoying.

Now and then the announcer gave his name and said he was "spinning the platters". For the next three years, he read the postcards and spun his platters, and I listened, but no "someone who knows" or "someone with a shoulder to cry on" or any other lovesick swain requested a romantic song for me.

My sister, Bev, requested "Good Night, Irene" by the Weavers for my mother. Her name was Irene, but she could barely tolerate that song. She was not amused. "Don't request another song for me," she warned. Bev thought "Slippin' Around" by Margaret Whiting would be fun to request for our proper Mother, but she thought better of it.

It didn't matter. The very act of tuning in to "my program" on "my radio" improved my self-image. I was part of something bigger than our farm and my family. I wasn't exactly worldly, but you might say I was ranging all over the county!

On Saturday I listened to "The Hit Parade". I'd try to guess the order of the songs, and it wasn't that hard. After all, I heard the same songs over and over all week on "my program".

My mother showed no interest in my four o'clock nightly indulgence. She worried about the batt'ry, and the only program she and my father listened to was the six o'clock news and the weather.

I was becoming more sophisticated by the day; my parents were not.

One Saturday, as I hovered over the radio, I heard the platter spinner play "I Went to your Wedding" by Patti Page. When he was finished, he said, "Thank you, Patti Page."

I couldn't believe it! Patti Page had come to Cortland!

I ran to the kitchen to tell my mother.

Unsophisticated as she was, Mother set me straight.

"I don't think so," she said gently. "He was just thanking her for singing such a lovely song, wherever she was."

Oh.

Without my mother's sophisticated outlook, I might have gone to school on Monday and said--oh, never mind.

TRIVIA

Questions:

1. Name one popular radio commercial

2. The old '78 records were made of shellac. What were the 45's made from?

3. The 7" 45's made their appearance in the late sixties. What famous British singing group made their appearance during that decade?

Answers:

1. Rinso White, Cheerios (The Lone Ranger) Halo Shampoo, Chesterfield Cigarettes

2. Vinyl

3. The Beatles

SINGIN' FOR THE GOOD OL' LIFEBUOY

When I was seven and the twins were nine, our sister, Jessie, married a young dairy farmer. As soon as they set up housekeeping in a tenant house on his property, Jessie invited us three little sisters to come for a visit.

We were thrilled to find that Jess had electricity and a console radio with a small amber-colored window and a light so Jess could see to tune the dial. We weren't as interested in "Helen Trent" or "Bob McNeil's Breakfast Club" as we were in the advertising jingles, and we tuned our ears to listen every time one came on. For some reason, we thought that, by knowing the words to them, we could launch ourselves into the modern world.

Every evening, after chores, our brother-in-law loaded his cans of milk into the back of his truck and drove up the road, through the little town of Cincinnatus, and to the Borden plant, where he delivered his milk.

"You kids want to ride up with me?" he asked.

We looked at each other. Did we ever!

We loaded into the back of the truck with the milk cans and started off.

I don't know who got the idea that we should sing, but as soon as we started through the town we began singing every jingle we knew:

I'm a Chiquita banana, and I've come to say
Bananas have to ripen in a certain way

When they're flecked with brown and have a golden hue
Bananas taste the best and are the best for you . . .

M-m-m good
M-m-m good
That's what Campbell's soups are
M-m-m good

Double your pleasure
Double your fun
With double mint, double mint, double mint gum

Singing in the bathtub
Singing for joy
Singing for the good ol' Lifebuoy

Halo everybody Halo
Halo is the shampoo that glorifies your hair
So Halo, everybody Halo
Halo shampoo, Halo!

Nobody at our house drank beer, but we belted out that jingle, too:

What'll you have
Pabst Blue Ribbon
What'll you have
Pabst Blue Ribbon
What'll you have Pabst Blue Ribbon
Pabst Blue Ribbon beer!

Our voices flew out behind us as we bounced along, accompanied by the clanging and rattling of the milk cans. It was easy for me to pretend that we were "on the air", and maybe, in some way we were.

We sang our jingles every night, feeling so proud and modern. We were hip. We were "with it"!

Sometimes, when I think back on those times on the milk truck, I wonder what in the world the people in Cincinnatus must have thought when they heard us. They probably thought it was the silliest serenade they ever heard.

TRIVIA

Questions:

1. What served as billboards in the country?

2. How could farmers tell which milk cans were theirs?

3. Why did farmers include a jersey or Guernsey cow in their herd?

Answers:

1. Barns

2. They painted an identifying number on them

3. To raise the butterfat content in the milk, which increased its value

BOILER INSPECTOR
(A City Story by Jon)

In the nineteen forties, the trains wound through Binghamton, New York in a steady procession, day and night—passenger trains, stopping at the station and chugging away again, and freights trains, trundling slowly in and out of the yard.

Every night I'd lie in bed, listening to the busy banging and clanging, as workers coupled cars, putting trains together. Occasionally, a switch failed or some other mishap occurred, and I'd hear the boom of a torpedo. I could hear the cheery whistles of the passenger trains, too, as they approached and departed the station.

We lived about a mile away from all the excitement, close enough to trigger my imagination night after night. The sounds of the trains were better than any bedtime story.

A viaduct arched above the tracks near the passenger terminal, creating a bridge for the Chenango Street traffic. A person could stand on its sidewalk and look over the railings to study the tops of the railroad cars and the gleaming tracks, to listen to the chug-chug-chug of the mighty engines building steam, to smell the smoke, and to watch the sparks escape from the smokestacks. For a ten-year-old like me, always fascinated with fire, what could be better?

My mind hummed and whirred all the time, imagining the things I could do (and probably would) and never considering any consequences. Boys my age knew without being told, that, when you started considering outcomes and then abandoned your big plans, you didn't get anything done.

That's why, one day, it occurred to me that, if I positioned myself precisely along the railing, I'd be able to look down the smokestack of one of the passenger trains and see straight into its roaring furnace as it emerged from the viaduct.

My friend, Bob Sage, and I walked the mile and a half to my lookout point.

I heard the train roll slowly away from the station—a passenger train, chugging softly, building steam, as it headed west under the viaduct. I took my post, leaning over the railing as far as I dared, and waited for the engine to emerge. I had timed everything perfectly! Chug-chug—and then, just as my eyes came into perfect alignment with the smokestack—CHUG!!! The smokestack erupted in a violent cloud of hot acrid smoke, peppered with sparks. I shut my eyes and gasped for air as the force of it shoved me away from the railing. The train moved on down the track and gave a blast of its whistle, and then it was gone. I hadn't seen a thing.

The damage was substantial. My white tee shirt was black and shot through with holes from the sparks, and all my exposed skin was covered in soot. My eyes burned from the smoke, and I could taste it in my mouth and smell it in my nose.

Whatever happened after that has blessedly escaped my memory. I don't remember if my buddy Bob sustained any damage, I don't remember how it felt to walk home along a busy city street, looking like I had just emerged from the fires of Hell. I don't remember what my mother said when she saw me.

I do know that I never tried to look down the smoke-stack of a train again.

TRIVIA

Questions:

1. Name two railroad lines
2. What is a hotbox?
3. Who collected tickets on passenger trains?

Answers:
1. DL&W, Burlington, Georgia Pacific . . .
2. An overheated axle or journal box on a rail car
3. The conductor

HAND ME DOWNS

Every year, about a month before school started, my mother began to assemble our school wardrobes. My sisters, the twins, and I stood before her in slips, shoes and socks, while she pulled our last-year's school dresses over our heads, tied their sashes, and buttoned their buttons. If there was any possible way, mother altered them so we could wear them for another year.

She lowered hems, reset buttons, covered small tears or stains with embroidery or appliqué, and let down the sleeves of our coats. Then she arranged the clothes on the bed, sorted by owner.

"Oh, now, look at you!" my mother would say, smoothing her hand over my collection of clothes. "You've got six lovely dresses!"

I was less than thrilled. The twins were two years older than I, and they generally wore identical dresses. That meant that my "six lovely dresses" were really three nice dresses, with three more just like them. Where were the garage sales when I needed them? Where were the clothing banks? When I was in kindergarten, I owned two red snowsuits with pointed hoods, two pairs of black buckled boots, four sets of winter underwear from Sears called "Comfy togs" and four pairs of long brown stockings. When I slipped into those hand-me-downs I wasn't sure who I was; I wasn't quite myself, but I wasn't quite one of the twins, either.

By the time I was ready to begin first grade, World War II was under way, and a great wave of support for our country and its war heroes spread across the land. Even my mother got caught up in it. Her little girls, she decided, would be pictures of patriotism on the first day of school. She sent an order to Sears: Eight yards of navy fabric printed with white stars, twenty-four white star-shaped buttons, and three yards of red ribbon.

When the package came from Sears, mother set to work, cutting, fitting, pinning, and finally, sitting at her Singer treadle sewing machine, transforming the pattern pieces into three patriotic symbols of perfection.

The twins and I paraded proudly down the hill to meet the bus that first day wearing star spangled sailor dresses, replete with big collars and perky red ties. Star-shaped buttons marched crisply down their fronts.

How fashionable I felt! How innocent I was! I was so pleased with my dress and my new saddle shoes and socks, I didn't give a thought to the disaster that would befall me two years later. By that time, I'd have outgrown my sailor dress, and then—oh, lucky me—I'd inherit two more from the twins.

To make matters worse, by the time I inherited those dresses the war was over, and sailor dresses were out of fashion. That didn't matter to my mother. According to her, they were fine, serviceable dresses, and, because she was able to let down the hems, I wore them for two more years.

TRIVIA

Questions:

1. Silk stockings were scarce during the war. What did women wear instead?

2. Why were new shoes so important?

3. Speaking of patriotism—what did school children gather to make kapok (used for military life preservers)

Answers:

1. Leg makeup

2. They were rationed

3. Milkweed

AUTOGRAPH BOOKS

Mostly, autograph books were "girl" things, often Christmas gifts, but plenty of young men got roped into writing in them. My big sisters' boyfriends wrote in mine, each of them using a whole page to write their names in tiny letters. They were not inspired contributors.

My dad wrote: "Roses are red, violets are blue, pickles are sour, and so are you."

My brother wrote: 'By hook or by crook, I'll be the last one to write in your book'.

My sisters wrote: 'When you get married and have a Ford, give me a ride on the running board', and 'Two in a hammock, attempting to kiss, and in a moment, they were just like this'. My mother wrote: 'Round is a ring that has no end, and so is my love for you, my friend'.

Friends wrote: 'I went to the movies tomorrow, and sat in the front of the back. I fell from the pit to the gallery and broke the front of my back. The band struck up but didn't play, so I sat down and walked away.' Another friend wrote, 'The deer love the valley, the fox love the hill, Laura loves the boys and I guess she always will."

Oh, those little rhymes were so entertaining—so un-original! Even today, I think I remember every one of them.

We weren't the inventors of autograph books, how-ever. I have my grandmother's—an ornate velvet-covered treasure, with "ALBUM" scripted across its front in silver letters. The year was 1883, and people couldn't seem to think of anything uplifting to write. Her brother wrote: "Be gentle, kind, and good, and remember your brother far away in the Pennsylvania woods." Another brother wrote: 'May your cares all fly away like dew before the sun, and when you have nothing else to do, think of me for fun.'

The autographs go down hill from there:

A friend wrote: 'In friendship let us live, in friendship let us die, and meet each other in a land beyond the sky." A gloomy friend named Daisy wrote:

'On your cheek the rose is blooming, health is sparkling in your eye. But remember, dearest Annie, God has said we all must die.'

Well, thank you, Daisy! What dour words for my twelve-year-old grandmother!

For some, life seemed jollier. From an 1893 book:

'Fall into the sea from off the deck, Fall into the ditch and break your knee, Fall from the shining height above, But never, never fall in love.'

'Beware of the boys.' (Advice from a brother)

'Roses are red, Sunflowers are yellow, And you are the one who stole my fellow.'

'When on this page you chance to look, Turn it over and close the book.'

'When you stand up to get married, and the minister says "obey", You just say I shan't do it, and see what the minister will say.'

'When you are tired of life, And all its busy scenes, go out into the garden and hide behind the beans.'

'Beware, beware of young man's love, Don't place your trust upon it, For seldom is it strong enough to buy you a new bonnet.'

'Long may you live, happy may you be, sitting in the woodpile, drinking catnip tea.'

Here are a few from the 1940's and World War II:

'May all your paths be strewn with roses, and all your kids have pug noses.'

'I don't seem to be able to think because my mind is on the blink.' (PFC Jack).

'In the parlor there were three, She, the parlor lamp and he. Three is a crowd, so they say, So the parlor lamp went out.'

'I love you, You love me, We gotta scram, Here comes an M.P.'

'Remember, Dear Clara, don't stay out late, and when you get home, don't stop at the gate.'

Sometimes, the early books provided a safe place for special papers. One contained brief, sympathetic notes from the director of a mental institution detailing the condition of a woman's brother. The outlook was always the same—he had "put on flesh" but there was no improvement.

Another book from 1884 contained a cure for baldness:
"How to Keep The Hair From Falling Out"
2 oz. castor oil, 4 grains carbonate of potash, 2 drachmas tincture canthris, 2 oz. alcohol. Shake well before using and brush the hair every night with a good clean brush."

The book had belonged to a woman, but I like to think the concoction was intended for her husband.

For the most part, though, autograph books were just plain fun, and the sillier the messages, the better we liked them.

Some of those rhymes are so common, everybody knows them. Do you remember these?

TRIVIA

Questions:

1. When you get married and have twins, don't come to my house for ......

2. Down by a little stream carved on a rock, are these little words: Forget ....

3. When you are old and cannot see, put on your specs and think ....

Answers:
1. Safety pins
2. Forget me not
3. Of me

STEALING FROM SEARS ROEBUCK

A neighbor was moving, and she needed help with her packing.

Our family enjoyed a "busy bee" reputation, so the woman drove up to our house to hire a girl. My sister, Jess, the busiest of busy bees in our family, volunteered to help.

After working hard for two days, she hurried home to tell our family what had happened.

The neighbor was packed and ready to go, with the furniture and a pile of boxes, carefully tied with string, waiting by the door. The house was empty, except for an old upright piano.

The neighbor looked around, pleased with what my seventeen-year old sister had accomplished. Then she said, "Jess, I want you to know how much I've appreciated your help, but I don't have any money to pay you."

Poor Jess!

"That's not fair!" she protested.

"No, it's not," the woman said, "I'll tell you what I'll do. I'll give you that piano. I can't move it, anyway."

"I'm sure you know Mr. Bronson," she continued. "I'll get him to truck it for you."

Mother was uncertain.

"Our floors are shaky," she said. "I'm not sure they'll hold a big piano.

"Sure they will," Dad said. "We can put it against that wall. It's got a good beam under it."

The next afternoon, our piano arrived unceremoniously in a rattling cattle truck. The driver helped Dad move it in.

When the truck had rumbled down the road, the nine-year-old twins and I, age seven, set to work. We dusted and cleaned the keys, including the one with the missing ivory. We polished the piano's case. My mother sorted through her box of photographs and selected some framed pictures of good-looking people. I didn't know some of them, but they looked just fine on the piano.

We were ready! Dad picked out "Red River Valley" with one finger to show us how it was done. Then, we took turns, trying to play our new acquisition. When Bea's turn came, she thoughtfully tried all the keys. Then she began to create chords. Then she could play whatever she wanted! Just like that! Bea was a natural!

When Bea learned to play, the three youngest busy bees left the hive and swarmed around the piano. Bea played, and all three of us sang. We sang every song we knew--songs we had learned at school, songs our father sang, and even old Civil War songs that we had learned from our grandmother. We sang Christmas songs in July and "Easter Parade" in August. We sang train songs and songs about hobos and bums

Since we didn't have a radio, we couldn't keep up with the modern songs. One evening we couldn't think of a single song to sing. Bea reached with her left hand to the end of the keyboard, and played thunderous chords, hard and loud.

"I should think you two could at least think of songs," she grumbled. "After all, I play the piano."

Bev and I thought as hard as we could, but no songs came to us.

Then Bev had an idea.

"Get the Sears catalog," she said. "They sell records. We can sing their songs."

I was uneasy. "Isn't that stealing?" I asked.

Bev snorted. "Heck no. It's not as if we stole the records. Anybody can sing the songs."

"But . . .but . . . They want us to buy the records, not sing their songs."

"How do you think the catalog people will hear us singing way out here in the country?" Bea said. "Go ahead. Tell us."

I was stumped. The twins had won.

Bev began to read the record offerings:

"I'll Never Smile Again"

A crash of thunder erupted from the piano.

"Never heard of it," Bea grumbled.

"Paper Doll"

Another crash of thunder.

"Just get a pencil and mark the ones we know," Bea said."

Bev underlined thirteen selections of the twenty-six that were offered.

I felt better. We had left Sears Roebuck plenty of their songs, and we had some new ones to sing.

Oh, wait! I erased the line under "I Don't Want to Set the World on Fire" because when we started to sing it, we realized we only knew the first stanza.

Nevertheless, everyone was happy.

Bea was happy to have new songs to play. Bev was happy because she had thought of the catalog. I was happy because we had returned so many songs to Sears.

TRIVIA

Questions:

1. What size were the records Sears sold in 1940?
2. Who was the famous "Singing Cowboy"?
3. Name a famous group of sisters who sang in the '40's

Answers:

1. 78's

2. Gene Autry

3. Andrews sisters, McGuire sisters. Lennon sisters

BURMA-SHAVE

Today, a startling number of kids struggle with reading. They fuss along, jolting through the words, trying to make sense of those squiggles on the page that are called letters. Our kids need Burma-Shave. Who could resist those small red signs posted close to the road on the old two-lane highways? We were forced to read fast—no driver I ever knew slowed down so kids could read them, and there was no looking back if you missed one of the signs. Kids had to stay at the ready, too. Turn your head and you could miss a whole jingle.

The sign on Route 11 between Marathon and Cortland, New York said:

If you must test
Her pucker paint
Better drive
Where traffic ain't
Burma-Shave

If you were lucky enough to take a long trip, you could read Burma-Shave jingles all across the country. Okay. Get ready, now. Here they come

Substitutes would
irk a saint
You hope they
are
What you know
they ain't
Burma-Shave

College cutie
Pigskin hero
Bristly Kiss
Hero
Zero
Burma-Shave

All little rhyming
jokes aside
Don't be content
until you're tried
Burma-Shave

Put your brush
Back on the shelf
The darn thing
Needs a
Shave itself.
Burma - Shave

He's the boy
The girls forgot
His line
Was smooth
His chin was not
Burma-Shave

Give hand signals
To those behind
They don't know
What's in
Your mind
Burma-Shave

He married Grace
With scratchy face
He only
Got one day
Of Grace
Burma-Shave

A scratchy chin
Like bright
Pink socks
Puts a romance
On the rocks
Burma-Shave

Buy a jar
Take it from me
There's so much
In it
The last half's free
Burma-Shave

You can't reach 80
Hale and hearty
By driving 80
Home from
The party
Burma-Shave

Substitutes and
Imitations
Send them to
Your wife's
Relations
Burma-Shave

It's best for one
Who hits
The bottle
To let another
Use the throttle
Burma-Shave

Don't pass cars
On curve or hill
If the cops
Don't get you
Morticians will

Burma-Shave

Always remember
On any trip
Keep two things
Within your grip
Your steering
wheel &
Burma-Shave

The bearded devil
Is forced
To dwell
In the only place
Where they don't
sell
Burma-Shave

With glamour girls
You'll never click
Bewhiskered
Like a
Bolshevik

Burma-Shave

The folks at Burma-Shave didn't worry about whether kids could read and understand words like "morticians", "substitutes", "imitations", and 'bewhiskered'. It was up to us to figure it out. The signs supposedly weren't intended for smooth-faced children who had no use for such a product. Still, I can't imagine a dad in the thirties, forties, and fifties who didn't hear the Burma-Shave jingles read to him by young voices in the back seat.

How effective were those signs? They're considered some of the best advertising of all time!

TRIVIA

Questions:
Was Burma Shave a cream or a soap?
The signs were red. What color was the lettering?
How many signs were in a series?

Answers:
1. Brushless shaving cream
2. White
3. Five, including the last one—Burma-Shave

THE SCOOTER RIDE

Scooters are designed for city children to enjoy. Their tiny wheels whiz along on smooth sidewalks and driveways without a bump or a glitch. In the country, however, they're clumsy and slow and usually not very exciting for kids.

When a scooter arrived on our farm along with its visiting city owner, my eleven-year-old sister, Bev, and I, who was nine, were delighted. This was a city toy, and therefore, automatically imbued with magic. We couldn't wait to give it a test run--but where? Our front yard, and rough farm fields could grudgingly accommodate a bicycle, but a scooter didn't have a chance. Our dirt road was rough and stony, and for the first hundred yards it was perfectly flat. That meant lots of pushing.

After the flat stretch, the road dropped off steeply for another hundred yards and then twisted into a sharp curve before it dropped again for the long run to the county road. What a thrill it was to fly down that road in the winter! We jumped on our sleds and took off, dragging our feet to slow down a little before we barreled into the steep bend, then sped along the straightaway all the way to the bottom of the hill.

What kind of thrill would it be to fly down that hill standing upright on a scooter?

Bev thought we should try it.

She pushed our borrowed city toy along the flat section of our road, and then she stopped.

"You can go first," she said.

I studied the steep hill waiting for the scooter and me. I hesitated. Being the youngest kid in the family, I had been tricked and duped by my sisters, the twins, so many times I had grown wary.

My mother was strict about name-calling, but when the twins were out of her hearing range, they often resorted to words like 'fraidy cat, scaredy cat, crybaby, dumb dooney, and blat baby to manipulate my behavior: "Just do what we want you to do and quit crying," they said.

"Why don't you go first, Bev?" I said. "I need to watch you so I can see how to do it."

"There's nothing to it," she said. "Look at those little wheels. How fast could they possibly go? Just hop on and balance yourself and don't be such a scaredy cat."

Bev had said the magic word--scaredy cat.

Well, I was no scaredy cat. I'd show her.

Almost as soon as I pushed off and boarded the scooter I knew I had made a terrible mistake. I hadn't bothered to ask how to slow it down or stop it.

Too late. Those little wheels blurred with speed, kicking up stones and dust as they buzzed along. The weeds along the side of the road streaked past. Looming ahead was the curve. I'd never get around it.

I made the only decision I could--I had to jump off. I tried to steer toward the ditch where the weeds might cushion my fall, but the scooter was going so fast it tipped over as soon as I tried to turn the handlebars.

The scooter and I skidded along in the dust and gravel, and finally slid to a stop.

Cautiously I got to my feet, brushed off the dust, righted the scooter, and pushed it back up the hill.

My knees and elbows were bleeding, and tiny stones were imbedded in my hands.

Bev was waiting at the top of the hill, doubled over with laughter. As I limped toward her she gasped for breath and waved one hand helplessly in my direction.

"Oh! Oh! You looked so funny when you jumped off! Like a big dust ball rolling down the hill. So funny! You shoulda seen yourself!'

"It's your turn now," I said grimly. "By the way, I found the brake."

"Nah. I don't want to go," Bev said, bursting into another fit of laughter.

I pushed the scooter back to the house and washed the blood off my elbows and knees.

"Child," my mother said gently as she picked the gravel out of my hands with a needle, "Why would you try such a thing when you didn't even know how to ride it?"

"I'm no 'fraidy cat, I said.

"Ah," she said. "Which one of your sisters talked you into this?"

Bev was hovering behind mother, her eyes twinkling with mischief, and her hand over her mouth to hold back her laughter.

"Nobody talked me into it," I said, knowing that if I told the truth, I'd be a tattletale.

TRIVIA

Questions:
1. Where was the brake on a scooter?
2. What was the standard color for a scooter?
3. Give a brand name of a scooter

Answers:
1. In front of the rear wheel
2. Red
3. Radio Line (a branch of Radio Flyer) or "Mobo"

CLOTHESLINE TENTS

The twins and I have just nicely settled into our clothesline tent with our coloring books, crayons, puzzles, and games when we're summoned to the tent opening.

"Mail for the tent people!" my sister calls.

The three of us crowd to the opening of our shaky new dwelling and hold out our hands.

Doris, one of our big sisters, delivers folded scraps of paper. We retreat into the hot dim interior of our temporary home, carefully observing the rules of tent life: Stay away from the sides. You could bring the tent down. Don't go outside. You could bring the tent down. Don't fight over the crayons. Mom or a big sister might hear you, and they might take the tent down.

We sit in a circle in the middle of the tent and read our mail: "I love you", "You are a good girl", and, "I hope you like your tent."

I'm only five and not yet able to read, so the seven-year-old twins read my notes to me. Had I been able to write, I'd have responded: "I love you, too." "I know I'm a good girl," and "I love the tent!"

By childhood standards, clothesline tents are flawless. By adult standards, they're far from perfect. Any structure consisting of two quilts held together on the clothesline with clothespins is doomed to collapse. Besides, clotheslines always sag under the weight of quilts, reducing the headroom inside the dwelling to two or three feet. Then, there's the problem of ventilation.

Quilts are designed to provide warmth, and that's what they do, especially when they're pressed into service as a tent on a hot summer day. Combine that problem with limited openings at either end, and these tents are positively stifling.

Why, then, do flushed, sweaty-faced kids love them?

Some children like the idea that a tiny flimsy tent limits the size of occupants and guests. Moms, dads and older siblings can't fit in.

Keep out, big people! Children who believe in this idea forget the story of the big bad wolf.

Others relish the special smells of a clothesline tent.

In its hot, dim interior, its occupants can savor the scent of the bruised grass that serves as the floor, the wooly infusion of the hot quilts, and the intoxicating perfume of warm Crayolas, waiting to be applied to a coloring book.

Of course, all kids love the special attention afforded clothesline tent dwellers.

A big sister or your mother takes the time to construct it. Someone who loves you delivers mail, and . . .

"Snack for the tent dwellers!" Doris calls.

The twins and I crowd to the opening of the tent again and hold out our hands.

Doris delivers cups of water and bread and butter sandwiches. We retreat back into the tent and enjoy our delicious little party.

Tent life lasts for about an hour. Then a restless occupant stretches a cramped leg, the clothespins give way, and down come the quilts. Or somebody sits on somebody else's crayon and breaks it, and there's a little squabble, and the clothespins give way. Or the dog pushes in, wagging his tail, and the tent people find themselves in a heap of quilts, exposed to the world and homeless.

A big sister comes and helps us fold up the quilts, and we put away our toys.

The outside air is warm and fresh and filled with sunlight. We can run and stretch and climb the apple tree in the yard, help ourselves to the sour fruit of the currant bushes, or make pretend tea from ragweed seeds. The possibilities are endless, and freed from the confines of the tent, we're ready to take on the world.

After a few days, however, we're ready for another clothesline tent. They're more fleeting than summer and childhood itself, and we need to enjoy them while we can.

TRIVIA

Questions:
1. Name three quilt patterns
2. What was the purpose of a clothes pole?
3. In most households, what day was designated as washday?

Answers:
1. Crazy quilt, Ducks Foot in the Mud, Double Wedding Ring, China Plate, Postage Stamp
2. It boosted up the clothesline
3. Monday

PUNCH BOARDS
(A city story by Jon)

During the Second World War, my dad was the fore-man in the machine shop at Lestershire Spool & Bobbin in Johnson City, NY. The company had a government contract to make spools for parachute cords.

There were several reasons why I loved to hop on the city bus after school and go down to visit my dad. First, I loved to be around him, to watch him standing at a milling machine or a lathe in his shop apron, cigarette dangling from his mouth, turning handles, measuring with his micrometers and verniers, making machine adjustments, always intent on his work. Second, sometimes he let me watch a lathe working, and on a long pass, at a certain point, he let me disengage the feed. I planted my ten-year-old feet on the worn wooden floor, just like my dad, while I inhaled the exotic warm oily smells of the place and got a feel for what he was doing.

Third, my dad bought chances on punchboards.

These colorful, easy-to-play gambling games were popular during and after World War II. People paid their money and chose a covered hole to punch out. Behind the hole was a rolled or folded slip of paper that revealed your prize, if you were lucky enough to win one.

These boards were little moneymakers for candy and cigar stores, cafes and taverns. A board that cost the propri-etor four dollars, beckoning players to buy a nickel punch could bring in a profit of around fifty dollars. Some boards cost as little as a penny per punch, or as much as a quarter, depending on the prizes offered. A twenty-five dollar jackpot wasn't unusual for a nickel punchboard.

Sometimes, my dad won a quarter, or even a dollar, or rarely, twenty-five dollars, which he could collect right away. Because of the war shortages, though, he'd have to wait for the Union Cigar Store to get its small allotments of candy bars and cigarettes. By the time the candy bars were available, Dad might be owed twenty or more. Sometimes he collected a whole carton of cigarettes.

It was my job, as I passed the cigar store on my way from the bus stop to Lestershire Tool and Bobbin to stop by and see if any of Dad's prizes had come in. When Dad won cigarettes, I'd hurry to the machine shop and hand them over, but delivering those candy bars, knowing Dad would pass most of them on to me, was about as close to heaven as a kid could get.

Sometimes, though, hiding behind the picture of Paul Bunyon and Babe, his blue ox or Adolph Hitler ("Take a punch at Hitler!" the punch board said) or a gorgeous pin-up girl, a gambler might find a slip of paper good for a bottle of beer or a Coke, or even a Zippo lighter.

Or---

Talk about a lucky punch!

My dad won a ballpoint pen, an aluminum Reynolds, I think. Dad and I didn't know it, but the first shipment of those pens was heavily advertised at Macy's in New York for around twelve dollars each, and they sold out almost immediately. No doubt, those eager buyers discovered the same thing we did--it was, after all, a brand new product, and it was in dire need of perfecting.

"Here, Jon," Dad said. "Try it out."

At first, I couldn't make a single mark. Dad pressed down hard with it, and away it went. Did it ever! There was no stopping it. It left smears and clots on the paper and on me.

In no time at all, my hands were stained with ink. It left its mark on the table where I put it down, and it stained my pocket when I tried to carry it with me.

Dad tossed the pen away.

Now, I wish I had kept it. It was a first, fumbling attempt to make something brand new, and with a bit of tinkering, it changed the writing world forever.

TRIVIA

Questions:

1. What famous man was a salesman for punchboards?

2. Punch boards were popular for advertising certain products. Estimate how many Zippo lighters were sold through punchboards from 1934-1940.

3. Most states have outlawed punchboards, except for what purpose?

1. Jack Ruby, who killed Lee Harvey Oswald, President Kennedy's assassin

2. 300,000

3. Fundraisers

A KINDERGARTEN EDUCATION

On my first day of school, I walked carefully down-stairs and into the kitchen, stroking the front of my green and white dress, feeling the silky smoothness of the starch. I was lovely. I was perfect. I was so excited I could barely breathe. Mother pinned a dishtowel around my neck to protect my beautiful dress while I ate breakfast, and my sister, Jessie, brushed my hair.

I walked out the door with my sisters, into a golden September day.

We waited beside our mailbox and watched for the tan and dark green bus to crest the hill from our neighbor's. Then, Jess started giving me instructions.

"We're bus number five," Jess said. Remember that, okay? Bus number 5."

She put her arm around my shoulders.

"See the number five on the bus?"

I nodded and climbed aboard.

A glance at the driver, looking serious and owl-like in his glasses, a quick left turn, and there I was, facing more kids than I had ever seen in my life, a blur of them in all shapes and sizes, and Jessie pushing on my back. Were they all looking at me? I felt my face getting hot, felt the shaky embarrassed smile that I hated take over my face.

"Here," Jess said, turning my shoulders toward a seat. "Why don't you sit by the window so you can see the other kids get on?"

The bus lurched forward, and we rattled down Pine Hill and turned onto the smooth county road. I looked back to see if I could find our house, but the fog hovered outside the bus window like a soft gray feather tick. On Pine Hill the sun had been shining.

When Number Five turned in at the school, Jess said, "Look quick! There's your room! Did you see it?"

I didn't. I was watching the line of buses winding around the driveway like a giant caterpillar, and kids rushing through the school doors and disappearing into the big brick building.

Jess pushed me ahead of her, and we stepped off the bus.

My sister. Shirley was waiting for me.

"Come on," she said. "I want to show you something."

I trotted beside her, holding tight to her hand as we made our way through the throng of children.

She took me into the girls' room and opened one of the grey doors in the row of them opposite the sinks.

"This is a real toilet," she said. "Pull down your pants and go."

I stared down into the sparkling white bowl. It looked as clean as any dish in our pantry.

"What if I have to poop?"

"Just poop and then use this paper. Tell me when you're done and I'll show you how to flush it."

I pulled the little handle and watched my deposit disappear and water swirl in.

"How do you turn it off?"

"You don't," she said. "It stops by itself."

She showed me how to turn the water on in the sink, push the plunger on the soap dispenser, and help myself to a paper towel.

"Come on," she said. "I'll show you something else."

Shirley looked both ways when we went out in the hall, and then she opened the door to a closet filled with stacks of paper. We went in. It was dark in there, and Shirley left the door open a crack.

"See that string hanging down? Pull on it. Don't yank it, whatever you do."

Carefully I pulled the string and the single bulb high above my head turned on.

"Pull the string again," Shirley said.

I turned off the light, but I held onto the string.

"Shut the door!" I said.

I pulled the string, and the paper closet filled with light.

"Open the door!"

"I pulled the string, and the light turned off.

"Shut the door!"

"That's enough," Shirley said. "Now, I'll take you to your room. Don't tell the other kids what I showed you. They already know."

That afternoon, when the bus had dropped us off at our mailbox, I watched it trundling down the hill in a cloud of dust. As soon as it was out of sight, I crossed my legs and hopped around in front of my sisters. The bumpy bus ride had taken its toll on my bladder.

"Lettuce turnip and pee!" I gasped.

"Well, pull down your pants and go," Shirley said.

I pulled down my panties and squatted.

"Pee in the middle of the road, get a sty on your eye," Jessie said.

I scuttled to the side and watered some grass.

Then I sprinted away from my sisters and rushed up the hill to tell my mother all my big news.

"Tell-The-News! Little Miss Tell-The News!" the twins yelled.

I didn't care. I had big news to tell my mother, about toilets that flushed and lights that turned on just by pulling a string, and I needed to tell her before the other kids rushed in.

TRIVIA

Questions:

1. "Pee in the middle of the road"--name two other warnings that children believed

2. Kindergartners were treated to snacks every afternoon, and the beverage was always a small bottle of milk. How did the children prepare their milk?

3. How were the little bottles sealed?

Answers:

1. Step on a crack break your mama's back, break a mirror, seven years bad luck . . .

2. They shook it to distribute the cream

3. With cardboard discs

FIRST AID

Since we were a hardy bunch, our family didn't have a big supply of first aid items. "Real" first aid materials were kept on a narrow shelf behind the pantry door. Other medications were multi-use, and they were stored where they were used the most often.

Here is a list of our first aid supplies, what they were used for, and my evaluation of their usefulness:

Medication	Purpose	Evaluation
Camphorated Oil	Rub on chest for colds	Oily, stinky, doesn't work. Try not to cough in front of your mother
ExLax	Treat toilet troubles	Boy, does it ever
Blackberry juice	Treat diarrhea	Delicious and effective. Bring it on!
Poultices	Treat cuts and boils	Wet and messy, but they work
Spearmint tea	Treat belly aches	Very tasty. Of course it works.
Powdered alum	Treat canker sores	Heated to bubbling and applied hot to canker sore. Don't tell if you have a canker sore, or if you do tell, prepare to run for your life
Oil of cloves	Treat tooth ache	Soothing, but you still have a bad tooth
Baked onion	Treat earaches	Warm juice is squeezed in ear. Smelly.

Doesn't work

Baked potato	Treat earaches	Isn't smelly, but it doesn't work
Warm cigarette smoke	Treat earache	Doesn't work
Turpentine	Treat cuts	Doesn't sting. Works for horses or kids
Spring Tonic	Sulphur & Molasses	Run for your life
Kerosene	Treat lice	Could catch hair on fire. Doesn't work
Bed on two chairs	Treat lonely sick child	Push two kitchen chairs together, add two bed pillows and a blanket, place sick child on the bed in the kitchen. Lovely! Very effective!

TRIVIA

Questions:

1. Medications were changing quickly during the war. What new drug was available during earlyWWII?

2. What drug became available to the military just before the Normandy invasion?

3. What defines Patent Medicine?

Answers:

1. Sulfa

2. Penicillin

3. They're usually protected by copyright instead of a patent

THE CHRISTMAS RING

Winter came early in 1945, the year I was nine and my sisters, the twins, Bev and Bea, were twelve. The first big snow arrived in mid November, and after that, the storms just kept coming, practically piling on top of each other, riding the shrieking north winds down from Canada. Our isolated farm in New York State was perched at the top of a hill on a dirt road. The house and barn were surrounded by open meadows, so the wind had its way with us, blowing the snow into nearly impassable drifts. Sometimes, we'd wait for days for the town plow to chug up our hill, pushing aside the snow with its great red wings and inviting us into the world again.

On the days when there was school, Dad hitched up the team and we children climbed into the sledge and rode through the snow, down to the plowed county road where we caught the school bus. In the afternoon, Dad would be waiting to take us home, When we arrived at our mailbox he removed one thick mitten long enough to pick up the day's mail and an occasional package, which he handed to one of the twins under the horse blankets. Then he coaxed the team back up the hill through the drifts. We spent the evenings reading, doing homework, listening to our old house creak in the wind, and peering out at the snow.

My grown-up sisters and my brother always came for Christmas with their spouses and little kids, bringing popcorn balls wrapped in red and green cellophane, cookies, candies, nuts, pies, and red Jell-O, and presents for everybody in the family. What a day it was! The men, including Dad, retreated to the living room where they circled the parlor stove in their wooly sock feet and caught up on manly news. The women bustled around in the kitchen, peeling potatoes and checking the turkey, stepping over creeping babies and around toddlers, and urging older kids to "go see your daddy". The dog took cover for the day, squeezing behind the kitchen stove.

Around the middle of December of that blustery year, with the winds still howling and the storms still on the attack, my older siblings worried that they'd be stopped by the storms. Even if the plow came by, cars couldn't make it up our road. Carrying the food, babies, and presents up the hill in such terrible weather would be nearly impossible.

Thank goodness, nothing deterred the U.S. Post Office! Packages began to arrive beside the mailbox--cartons wrapped in brown paper and tied with string.

When Dad brought the first box home, Mother opened it and let us look inside. It was filled with brightly wrapped, beribboned gifts from our brother Dave.

"I'll put these presents away until Christmas," Mother said. "That way, you children won't be tempted to peek."

The next day, a box arrived from our city cousins. Again, Mother let us look inside. Those gifts from the land of streets and sidewalks, which we had never seen, carried a special excitement and glamour, even before we opened them.

Dad cut a Christmas tree and dragged it into the woodshed.

"You kids get the broom and brush the snow off, and then I'll bring it in the house," he said.

As usual, it was a hemlock with one flat side, which we cleverly placed against the wall. We decorated it with balls, garlands, ornaments, and homemade paper chains. Then, we hung well-used wreaths in the windows and paper bells from the living room ceiling. Despite the lack of lights, since we had no electricity, our house was beautiful.

In no time the tree filled the house with the heady aroma of Christmas. The glittering decorations, the cards arranged on the piano, and the steady stream of packages filled us with so much holiday spirit we were nearly bursting.

That afternoon, the mailman left another brown box. It was from our sister, Marge. Again, Mother opened it, let us take a peek, and prepared to put it away. Bev, however, had been thinking, and she had come up with an idea.

"Wouldn't those presents look beautiful under the tree?" she said. "We could sort them, too. See? We could put your gifts here, and Dad's there, and mine there, and Bea's next to mine, and Laura's right there. It would be so easy to hand them out on Christmas."

Mother hesitated.

"It's against my better judgment," she said, "They'll be such a temptation."

She hesitated again.

"Well, all right," she said, "Once you get them arranged, though, don't shake, squeeze, or even smell them again until Christmas."

"Don't worry. We won't," Bev assured her. "Christmas is all about surprises. We know that."

Merrily we piled the gifts under the tree—a regular blizzard of them, just waiting to be opened. The presents we received then—coloring books and crayons, construction paper, card games and puzzles, diaries with keys, writing paper, costume jewelry, socks, and dainty linen hankies—would be considered stocking stuffers today. To us, they were magical, mysterious treasures that grew more tempting with each day.

As the days passed, Mother grew more uneasy about trusting us with the presents. Every night, she put on her hat and coat, gathered up her lantern and pail, and went to the barn to help with the milking. Now, she began to pause at the kitchen door and remind us sternly, "Don't touch those presents!"

"Don't worry. We won't," we assured her.

Angels that we were, we obeyed for several nights. Then, one evening as we stood around the tree admiring our Christmas mysteries, Bea said, "What if we peeked at just one? How about that odd-shaped box that doesn't rattle when I shake it?"

Bea opened three pairs of socks. What a disappointment! She wrapped them back up and tried again. Her second selection was much better--three jigsaw puzzles starring Henry of funny paper fame.

That night, we were small-time offenders, but by the next night, we had become stealthy big-timers. Opening those presents was a slow, delicate process, like cracking a safe. They were sealed with tape and tied tightly with ribbons. Since we didn't own more tape or ribbon, we had to take care that we could get the presents re-wrapped. Of course, like all good criminals, we grew more clever as we practiced, and in a few nights, we were opening everything, even inspecting Dad's new flannel shirts and gray wool socks and Mother's new nightgowns and cotton stockings,

The following week, a package arrived from our sister, Dot. Her gifts were covered with warning stickers: "Do Not Open Until Christmas!" The twins and I looked at each other. It was almost as if she knew what we had been doing.

As Bev placed her gift under the tree she said, "I know this is a ring. What else could it be in such a little box?"

"Put it with your pile of presents and leave it alone," Mother said. "Today isn't Christmas."

That evening while Mother was at the barn, Bev carefully opened her tiny package from Dot.

"I know what this is," she said, "But I need to open it to see what kind of a ring it is."

It was beautiful. Bev was thrilled. She slipped it on her finger and admired its yellow stone glistening in the lamplight. She turned her finger this way and that so Bea and I could appreciate the full effect.

Then Bea said, "Come on, Bev. Take it off and get it wrapped up before Mom comes."

Bev tried to slip the ring off her finger, but it wouldn't budge.

"Come on!" Bea and I prodded. "Hurry up!"

Bev put her finger in her mouth and gripped the ring tightly with her teeth. She pulled as hard as she could. The ring didn't budge.

Her finger was turning red and beginning to swell.

Bea rubbed Bev's finger with lard. Bev pulled and twisted, but the ring didn't come off. We tried soap. Bev pulled again, but with every attempt, her finger swelled a little more, and the ring was tighter than ever.

The clock was ticking. Mother would be coming back from the barn any minute.

Then, Bea had a brainstorm. Without a word, she grabbed a cup and raced outside. When she returned, she was carrying a cupful of snow. She took Bev's poor swollen finger and plunged it in.

"Keep it in there until I say you can take it out," Bea commanded. "And you"— she pointed her finger at me— "You stand by the window and let me know when you see Mom coming."

Finally, I saw the tiny yellow dot of Mother's lantern emerging from the barn.

"She's coming!" My words came out in a panicked squeak.

Bea took Bev's half-frozen finger out of the snow. The swelling was gone. Bea applied some soap, and miracle of miracles, the ring slipped off. Bev wrapped it up and placed it back under the tree just as we heard Mother stomping the snow off her boots in the woodshed.

I'd like to say we never peeked at Christmas gifts again, but after we perfected our stealthy skills that Christmas we couldn't seem to stop. For several years we made peeking a Christmas ritual. Then, age and maturity entered our lives, and our careers as small-time criminals came to an end.

TRIVIA

Questions:

1. Countrymen wore boots with liners in the winter. What material were they made from?

2. Women wore loosely knitted coverings over their heads. What were they called?

3. What was a muff?

Answers:

1. Felt

2. Fascinators

3. A thick tubular piece of fabric or fur with openings on each end to accommodate your hands

THE LESSON OF THE FLASHLIGHT

The twins were ten and I was eight the Christmas that Dad got the flashlight.

We were busily opening jigsaw puzzles, wooden animal pins to wear on our coats, construction paper, Archie comic books, coloring books, and paper dolls, and trying on new pastel-colored socks. None of us paid attention to what Dad was opening. His Christmases were dull compared with ours--he got gray wool socks with red stripes, plaid flannel shirts, long underwear, and heavy mittens—the same presents every year.

It wasn't until bedtime that Bev took a sudden interest in the flashlight.

"You look really tired tonight," she said to Mother.

"Christmas is a long day for us grown-ups," Mother said. "Of course, I'm tired when it's over."

"We could save you the trouble of leading us up to bed with the lamp tonight," Bev said kindly. "We could just take Dad's new flashlight and light our own way upstairs."

Mother hesitated.

"Do you know how to work it?" she asked.

"Oh, sure," Bev said. "Look. Push this button forward, and it turns on. Push it backward, and it turns off. That's all there is to it."

"Well, all right. Go ahead," Mother said, putting the kerosene lamp back on the table. "I'll go finish the dishes."

Bev carried the flashlight, Bea brought an armful of coloring books, new crayons, and comic books, I got the jigsaw puzzles and paper dolls, and we climbed the stairs.

Quickly, we slipped into our long flannel nighties and crawled into bed with our Chrismas bounty, including Dad's flashlight. Then, we made a teepee under the quilts and settled down to play.

How clever we were! Mother would never know her good little daughters weren't fast asleep!

We played until we were tired, and then we turned off the flashlight and went to sleep.

The next night, Mother said we could use the flashlight to light our way upstairs again. Again, we made our tent and selected our evening's entertainment. We hadn't played long when the bright beam of the flashlight began to turn a dull orange.

"I think it needs a rest," Bev said. Quickly, she turned it off and put it on the dresser. We understood how to turn it off and on, and now we were about to learn about batteries. For all we knew they could have a life of ten days or ten years. We certainly expected that the flashlight would serve our purposes for more than a night, especially if we gave it a long rest.

The next morning, we awoke bright and perky, and we expected the same of the flashlight. But when we turned it on, there was no light left in it at all.

It was time to give the flashlight back to Dad.

Dad pushed the switch back and forth a few times and pronounced that we had completely run down the batteries. Then, he put it on the pantry shelf. He hadn't had a chance to enjoy his Christmas gift, and, since he didn't have any spare money for new batteries, he wouldn't enjoy it anytime in the near future.

Still, he didn't scold us. I don't think there was a word for the lesson we learned that Christmas in the nineteen forties. Now, I think it would be called a "learning experience".

Trivia
Questions
1. Name a flashlight brand from the 1940's or 50's
2. Name a battery brand from any era
3. What were the outsides of a flashlight made from?

Answers
1. Ray-O-Vac, Duracell, Eveready
2. Energizer, Duracell, Eveready
3. Metal, rubber